Prais

BUILDING YOUR ART BUSINESS

"As president of the Livingston Arts Association, I've seen how important it is for artists to understand the business side of their craft. *Building Your Art Business* provides clear, actionable steps for growing an art career without sacrificing creativity. Whether you're a seasoned artist or just starting out, this guide is packed with invaluable tools and strategies."

—Marilyn Kalb, President,
Livingston (NJ) Arts Association

"Evan's passion for helping other artists is evident in *Building Your Art Business.* As an artist myself, I know how challenging it can be to navigate the world of marketing and promotion. Evan's book offers clear, practical guidance on everything from building a brand to selling art, both online and in-person. This is a must-read for artists looking to take control of their art careers."

— Marcia Miele Branca, Award-Winning Artist

"*Building Your Art Business* is an invaluable resource for artists at any stage of their career. Evan Stuart Marshall provides practical, actionable advice that will help artists not only navigate the business side of the art world but also thrive creatively. His deep insights into marketing, sales, and new media make this book a must-read for anyone looking to grow their art practice and reach a wider audience."

—**Barbara Sax,** President, Arts Council of Livingston (NJ)

"We had the pleasure of showcasing Evan's work in our gallery, and his creativity and professionalism left a lasting impression on us. Now, with *Building Your Art Business,* Evan has created an invaluable resource for artists looking to promote and sell their work. His insights are practical, accessible, and drawn from real-world experience. Whether you're an emerging artist or seasoned professional, this book is a must-have for navigating the business side of art."

— **Sally Harris and Ella Slayne,** Owners of Harmony Brookside Gift Shop & Gallery, Brookside, NJ

BUILDING YOUR ART BUSINESS

BY EVAN STUART MARSHALL

Artful Innovation Series

Abstract Art Revolution
Building Your Art Business
Collecting Abstract Art on a Budget

Building Your Art Business

MARKETING, SALES, AND STRATEGIES FOR SUCCESS

Evan Stuart Marshall

ESM Productions

esm.

ESM Productions
1 Pacio Court
Roseland, New Jersey 07068-1121
www.evanstuartmarshall.com

ISBN 978-1-0880-9834-9 (hardcover)
ISBN 978-1-0880-9857-8 (ebook)

Cover design © Evan Stuart Marshall
Book design by Evan Stuart Marshall

Illustration in Chapter 20:
Crumlish, Christian, 2021. Product Management
for UX People: From Designing to Thriving in a
Product World. New York: Rosenfeld Media
rosenfeldmedia.com/books/product-management-for-ux-people

To Martha

Contents

Introduction: The Business of Art

Building a career as an artist is not just about creating beautiful work—it's about getting that work seen by the right people and forging connections that lead to sales, recognition, and long-term success. In today's crowded and competitive art world, talent alone isn't enough. You need to think beyond the studio, and that's where art marketing comes in.

I wrote this book because, like many artists, I know what it's like to feel overwhelmed by the business side of art. As a self-taught artist, I learned to navigate the complexities of marketing and selling my work through trial and error, and I wanted to share that knowledge with others. My goal is to provide practical, actionable advice that helps you build a thriving art career without sacrificing your creative integrity. This book is a roadmap for artists who want to market their work, grow their brand, and take control of their artistic futures.

What is Art Marketing?

At its core, art marketing is about building connections. It's the process of promoting your work, creating visibility for yourself as an artist, and forming meaningful relationships with collectors, galleries, and your audience. Art marketing isn't about selling out or losing your artistic integrity—it's about ensuring that your work finds its way to people who appreciate it, value it, and are willing to invest in it.

Think of marketing as the bridge between your creative practice and the world outside. While creativity happens in the studio, marketing happens in the world beyond it. It includes everything from creating an engaging online presence and harnessing social media, to networking with gallery owners and hosting exhibitions. It's about telling your story as an artist and showing the world why your work matters.

Today, marketing is more accessible than ever, thanks to digital platforms and technology. Artists no longer have to rely solely on gallery representation or word-of-mouth. You can take charge of your marketing strategies, leverage online tools, and connect with potential buyers directly.

Marketing can also be an extension of your creativity. It's an opportunity to present your work in new, exciting ways. By applying the same passion and thoughtfulness to how you market your art as you do to your artwork itself, you can attract a loyal audience that shares your love for your work.

Why Marketing is Essential for Artists

You may be asking yourself, "Why do I need to focus on marketing? Isn't creating the art enough?" It's a common question, especially for artists who may feel marketing is outside their comfort zone. But no matter how talented you are, if people don't know about your work, it's difficult to build a sustainable career. Here are a few reasons why marketing is crucial for artists:

- **Visibility:** In the art world, visibility is everything. You could create masterpieces, but if no one knows they exist, you won't sell them. Marketing helps get your art in front of the right people—whether that's through social media, exhibitions, or online platforms.
- **Building Relationships:** Marketing is not just about selling individual pieces—it's about building lasting relationships with collectors, curators, galleries, and fans. Those who follow your work are often the ones who return to buy more, attend your exhibitions, and refer you to others. Marketing helps nurture these connections.
- **Consistency in Sales:** Effective marketing creates a steady stream of opportunities for selling your work. Instead of waiting for random sales or relying solely on galleries, marketing gives you the tools to actively reach your audience and sell directly to collectors and fans.

- **Establishing Your Brand:** Successful artists don't just sell art—they sell a story, a vision, and a brand. Marketing helps you build that brand. It allows you to communicate what makes your work unique, what your artistic message is, and why people should care. A strong brand sets you apart and makes your work more desirable.
- **Embracing New Technology:** The art world has changed dramatically over the last decade, with digital platforms becoming essential for connecting with collectors and fans. From Instagram to virtual exhibitions, artists are using technology to reach global audiences. In this book, you'll explore how to use these emerging tools to stay ahead in the evolving art market.

In this book, you'll learn how to develop a marketing strategy that aligns with your goals, your artwork, and your values. We'll dive into topics like building a strong online presence, using social media to engage your audience, and leveraging both online and offline tools to grow your art business. You'll also explore practical ways to diversify your income streams, from print-on-demand services to licensing, and how to make use of cutting-edge technologies like augmented reality (AR) and non-fungible tokens (NFTs).

Marketing might seem overwhelming at first, but with the right guidance, it can become an exciting and rewarding part of your artistic journey. You already have the creativity—now it's time to learn how to get your work out into the world.

1

The Business Plan

Creating a business plan for your art practice may not seem as exciting as making art, but it's essential for building a sustainable, successful career. A business plan acts as a roadmap, guiding you through setting goals, identifying opportunities, managing finances, and organizing the business side of your creative practice.

Creating a business plan for your art practice provides structure and direction. It helps you clarify your artistic goals, understand your market, and ensure that your business is sustainable. By outlining clear financial objectives, marketing strategies, and sales channels, you'll be able to build a thriving art career that reflects your vision and passion. By defining your artistic goals and understanding the structure of a business plan, you'll be better equipped to grow your art career and stay organized.

Defining Your Artistic Goals

Before you can create a business plan, you need to define your goals as an artist. These goals will shape the direction of your business and give you a clear vision of where you want to go.

Consider asking yourself the following questions:

- **What do you want to achieve in your art career?** Are you focused on selling your work, gaining gallery representation, growing an online presence, or something else? Be specific about what success looks like to you.
- **Who is your ideal audience?** Think about the type of people you want to connect with, whether they are art collectors, casual buyers, gallery owners, curators, or art enthusiasts.
- **What kind of artistic practice do you want to build?** Do you want to work in a studio full-time, travel and create on the go, or collaborate with other creatives? Knowing your desired working environment helps shape your business plan.

Having a clear set of goals gives you the direction you need to structure your business plan effectively. This plan should serve as both a practical guide and a source of motivation as you grow your art practice.

Creating a Traditional Business Plan

A business plan for an artist is structured similarly to a traditional business plan, with a few key adjustments to fit the creative industry. Here are the main sections you'll want to include, along with examples and advice specific to an art career:

Executive Summary

The Executive Summary is an overview of your art business. It introduces your goals, artistic vision, and how you plan to achieve them. This section is brief—typically one or two paragraphs—but it provides an essential snapshot of your plan.

In the Executive Summary, you should address:

- **Your artistic vision**: What do you create, and what themes do you explore in your work?
- **Your career goals**: Are you looking to sell more artwork, gain representation, or increase your online presence?
- **Financial objectives**: What income streams will you focus on (e.g., selling originals, prints, commissions, or teaching)?

Example:

"As a self-taught abstract artist, my goal is to build a sustainable career by creating and selling contemporary mixed-media works. I aim to increase my visibility through online platforms, secure gallery representation in key markets, and develop additional revenue streams, including limited-edition prints and commissions."

Company Description

This section describes who you are as an artist and what your art business entails. Think of it as your professional bio.

Here's what to include:

- **Your background**: Highlight your journey as an artist. Include key influences, training, and major career milestones.
- **What you create**: Describe your medium, style, and the themes your work explores.
- **What makes your work unique**: What sets you apart from other artists? Focus on the distinct elements of your process, subject matter, or technique.

Example:

"I am a mixed-media abstract artist specializing in bold, vibrant compositions that explore themes of identity and memory. Primarily self-taught, I have exhibited my work in both solo and group exhibitions across the U.S. My art draws inspiration from the natural world, and my signature technique involves layering found objects and acrylics to create textured, dynamic surfaces."

Market Analysis

Market analysis is crucial for understanding where your work fits in the art world. This section will help you identify your audience, understand your competition, and stay informed about trends in your market.

Here's what to include:

- **Target audience**: Describe the type of people who buy your work—collectors, art lovers, galleries, or interior designers.
- **Competitive landscape**: Analyze artists with similar styles or themes and how they market and sell their work. What can you learn from their strategies, and how can you differentiate yourself?
- **Trends in the art world**: Keep an eye on industry trends that affect demand for your type of art. For instance, are collectors increasingly buying art online? Are minimalist works in demand while abstract paintings are rising in popularity?

Example:

"My target audience consists of urban professionals aged 30–50 who are interested in contemporary abstract art. These collectors appreciate bold colors and textured compositions that evoke a sense of movement. I will focus on building relationships with both private collectors and interior designers who seek unique, statement pieces for residential and commercial spaces."

Marketing and Sales Strategy

Your marketing and sales strategy outlines how you will promote your art and sell it to your target audience. This is where you'll define the platforms and strategies you plan to use.

Key components of your marketing strategy:

- **Sales channels**: Where will you sell your work? Examples include your personal website, online galleries (such as Saatchi Art), Etsy, or in-person at art fairs and galleries.
- **Marketing tactics**: How will you market your art? Social media (Instagram, TikTok, Pinterest), email newsletters, blogging, and attending art fairs are all effective marketing tools.
- **Pricing strategy**: Describe how you will price your work. Will you use a pricing method based on size (e.g., height x width) or time spent on the piece? Be sure to align your pricing with your target audience.

Example:

"I plan to sell my work through a combination of online platforms, including my personal website, Saatchi Art, and 1stDibs, while also participating in local art fairs to connect with collectors in person. My pricing strategy will reflect the size and complexity of each piece, ensuring that my work remains accessible while maintaining its value."

Organizational Structure

Even if you're working solo, this section is important. It outlines how you will manage the various aspects of your art business.

Consider these questions:

- **Do you work with a gallery, agent, or manager?**
- **Do you have a support team?** (e.g., a photographer, marketing consultant, or assistant)
- **What roles will you take on yourself?**

This section helps you stay organized and clarify responsibilities, especially as your business grows.

Example:

"I manage all aspects of my art business, including creating the work, marketing, and handling sales. In the future, I plan to work with a social media assistant to streamline content creation and order fulfillment."

Financial Plan

The financial plan is the backbone of your business plan. This section outlines how much money you need to sustain your art practice and how you will generate revenue.

Here's what to include:

- **Startup and operational costs**: List your expected expenses, such as studio rent, art supplies, marketing costs, shipping, and exhibition fees.

- **Revenue projections**: Estimate how much money you plan to make from each income stream, whether from direct sales, commissions, teaching, or licensing.
- **Break-even analysis**: Determine how much art you need to sell each month to cover your costs. This will help you set realistic financial goals.

Example:

"I estimate my monthly expenses to be $2,000, which includes studio rent, materials, website hosting, and shipping costs. My revenue will come from a mix of selling original paintings, offering limited-edition prints, and teaching workshops, with a projected monthly income of $3,500."

Building a Sustainable Art Practice

Sustainability is key to building a long-lasting career as an artist. You'll need to ensure that your income streams are diverse and reliable, and that your work-life balance supports your creativity.

- **Diversify your income streams**: In addition to selling originals, consider creating prints, offering workshops, or licensing your work for commercial use. This ensures that you have multiple sources of income, reducing financial stress.
- **Manage your time effectively**: As an artist, it's important to balance time spent creating with time spent managing the business side of things. Scheduling

regular hours for marketing, networking, and sales tasks can help keep your business running smoothly without sacrificing studio time.

- **Track your progress**: Regularly review your financials, artistic goals, and marketing efforts to ensure you're on track. This will allow you to adjust your business plan as necessary.

Need some tools to help you develop your business plan or manage your time more effectively? Head to the **Practical Tools and Templates for Artists** section in the Appendix, where you'll find templates and resources to get started.

Action Points

- Define your artistic goals: What do you want to achieve with your art career?
- Write an Executive Summary that outlines your vision and career objectives.
- Describe your target audience and competitive landscape in the Market Analysis section.
- Develop a Marketing and Sales Strategy that includes both online and in-person channels.
- Create a financial plan, including your expenses, revenue projections, and break-even point.
- Regularly review and update your business plan to keep your goals and strategies aligned.

2

Defining Your Artistic Goals

In the art world, success is not just a matter of talent or creativity—it's about having a clear sense of purpose and direction. Defining your artistic goals helps you stay focused, motivated, and intentional in building your career. Whether you're an emerging artist figuring out your path or an established artist refining your practice, setting clear goals will guide your decisions and ensure that your creative work aligns with your larger aspirations.

Goals serve as a compass, helping you navigate the challenges and opportunities that come your way. By breaking down big dreams into actionable steps, you can turn vague aspirations into achievable milestones, providing clarity and structure to your artistic journey.

By defining your artistic goals, you establish a clear path

for your creative and professional growth. Your goals keep you grounded, focused, and motivated, while providing the structure necessary to navigate the ever-changing art world. Whether you're dreaming of your first solo exhibition or aiming to leave a lasting legacy, defining your goals will help you get there with intention and purpose.

Why Goal-Setting Matters for Artists

In any field, setting goals is critical, but for artists, it's especially important. The art world is often unpredictable, with no fixed path to success, making it easy to feel lost or uncertain about your next steps. Goals provide a sense of structure amid this uncertainty. They help you clarify what you want to achieve and create a roadmap to get there.

Some key reasons why goal-setting matters:

- **Direction and Focus**: Goals allow you to focus your time and energy on the things that matter most. Without goals, you may end up pursuing projects that don't align with your larger aspirations.
- **Accountability**: When you have clear goals, you can hold yourself accountable. It becomes easier to assess whether you're on track or if you need to make adjustments.
- **Motivation**: Working toward a specific goal gives you a sense of purpose and achievement. Whether it's finishing a new series, securing gallery representation, or

growing your online audience, each milestone brings a sense of accomplishment.

- **Progress Tracking**: Without goals, it's difficult to measure progress. Having clear objectives helps you evaluate your success and identify areas for growth.

Understanding Your Artistic Vision

Before you can set meaningful goals, you need to understand your artistic vision. This involves reflecting on what motivates and inspires you as an artist. Your vision is the foundation of your goals—it shapes the kind of art you want to create, the audience you want to reach, and the impact you want to have.

Ask yourself the following questions to clarify your vision:

1. **What themes or subjects are central to your work?** Do you find yourself drawn to certain ideas, such as nature, identity, social justice, or personal memory? Recognizing the recurring themes in your work will help you craft goals that are true to your creative voice.

2. **What are your core values as an artist?** Do you prioritize innovation, craftsmanship, activism, or aesthetic beauty? Understanding your values will help guide your artistic decisions, ensuring that your work remains aligned with what matters most to you.

3. **How do you want your audience to interact with your work?** Do you want viewers to engage

intellectually, be emotionally moved, or simply appreciate the aesthetics? Your goals should reflect the kind of experience you want to create for your audience.

4. **What is your artistic legacy?** Consider the impact you hope to leave behind. Are you aiming to challenge societal norms, preserve cultural traditions, or push the boundaries of your medium? Your long-term goals should encompass your vision for your artistic legacy.

The Power of SMART Goals

Once you've defined your artistic vision, it's time to translate that vision into actionable goals. A widely used framework for effective goal-setting is the SMART method, which ensures that your goals are:

- **Specific**: Clear, well-defined goals that leave no room for ambiguity.
- **Measurable**: Goals that can be tracked, allowing you to assess your progress.
- **Achievable**: Realistic goals that you can attain with your current resources and circumstances.
- **Relevant**: Goals that align with your broader artistic vision and long-term aspirations.
- **Time-bound**: Goals set within a specific timeframe to keep you accountable.

For example, instead of setting a vague goal like "I want to grow my audience," a SMART goal would be, "I want to increase my Instagram followers by 25% over the next three months by posting new content three times per week and engaging with other artists and collectors."

SMART goals help break down large, overwhelming tasks into manageable steps, making it easier to stay focused and motivated.

Balancing Short-Term and Long-Term Goals

Successful artists balance both short-term and long-term goals. Long-term goals reflect your broader vision for your career, while short-term goals are the immediate steps that will help you get there.

Long-term goals provide direction and a sense of purpose. They're the big-picture aspirations, such as:

- Establishing yourself as a leading figure in a specific artistic movement.
- Becoming financially independent through your art.
- Having a solo exhibition at a renowned gallery or museum.
- Gaining representation with a top gallery or being collected by prominent institutions.

However, focusing only on long-term goals can feel daunting. That's where **short-term goals** come in. These are the smaller, more immediate objectives that bring you closer to your long-term vision. For instance:

- Completing a new series of work within the next six months.
- Applying to five art residencies or exhibitions this year.
- Launching a website to showcase and sell your art.
- Learning a new technique or experimenting with a different medium.

The key is to break down your long-term aspirations into smaller, actionable short-term goals. This keeps you focused on what you can accomplish now, while maintaining momentum toward your larger vision.

Staying Flexible: Revisiting and Adjusting Goals

Goal-setting isn't a one-time exercise—it's an ongoing process. As your career evolves and new opportunities arise, your goals may shift. Flexibility is crucial, as the art world can be unpredictable. Be open to adapting your goals as needed.

For example, you may set a goal to have a solo exhibition within two years, but along the way, you might discover new opportunities for collaborations or online sales that take precedence. If your vision or circumstances change, don't be afraid to revisit and adjust your goals. This flexibility allows you to respond to opportunities without losing sight of your overarching vision.

Balancing Creative and Financial Goals

As an artist, one of the most important balancing acts is between creative fulfillment and financial sustainability. Creative goals often come from the heart—they're about artistic expression, exploration, and pushing boundaries. Financial goals, on the other hand, ensure that you can sustain your practice and thrive in the long term.

Creative goals might include:

- Developing a new body of work that reflects your evolving artistic voice.
- Experimenting with new materials, techniques, or subjects.
- Collaborating with other artists or participating in community art projects.

Financial goals could include:

- Generating a consistent income through art sales, commissions, or licensing.
- Building a steady client base or securing gallery representation.
- Diversifying income streams through print sales, teaching, or workshops.

It's important to set goals in both areas and to recognize that they can complement each other. By setting financial goals, you can create the stability that allows for greater creative freedom. Meanwhile, your creative goals keep your work authentic and exciting, which can, in turn, attract buyers and patrons.

Examples of Artistic Goals in Practice

To help illustrate how to set both short-term and long-term goals, here are some examples tailored to different stages of an artist's career:

Emerging Artist:

- *Long-term goal*: Establish a presence in your local art scene by exhibiting in three local galleries over the next two years.
- *Short-term goals*:
  - Develop a cohesive series of 10 paintings within the next six months.
  - Attend five local art networking events this year to meet gallery owners and fellow artists.
  - Set up an Instagram account focused on your work and post three times a week.

Mid-Career Artist:

- *Long-term goal*: Gain representation with an international gallery and expand your collector base abroad within five years.
- *Short-term goals*:

- ○ Create a new series that appeals to international markets.
- ○ Apply to at least five international art fairs and competitions over the next 12 months.
- ○ Establish an email list for collectors and galleries, and send quarterly updates on your work.

Established Artist:

- *Long-term goal*: Leave a lasting legacy by mentoring the next generation of artists and having your work featured in a major museum collection within 10 years.
- *Short-term goals*:
  - ○ Host one workshop or mentorship program for emerging artists each year.
  - ○ Apply for two residencies or fellowships that offer opportunities for public commissions.
  - ○ Collaborate with art schools or universities to teach a masterclass.

Accountability: How to Track Your Progress

Setting goals is the first step, but staying accountable is key to achieving them. Here are practical strategies to help you stay on track:

1. **Document Your Goals**: Write down your goals in a journal or use a project management tool like Trello

or Asana. Having a clear record of your goals will keep you organized and focused.

2. **Create a Timeline**: Establish deadlines for each goal. For example, set a goal to complete a new series by the end of the quarter, or to apply to a specific number of exhibitions by a certain date.

3. **Break It Down**: Large goals can feel overwhelming, so break them into smaller tasks. For instance, if your goal is to complete a new series of work, your tasks might include brainstorming ideas, purchasing supplies, and dedicating specific studio hours each week to work on the series.

4. **Review and Revise**: Set aside time every quarter or year to evaluate your progress. Have you met your short-term goals? Are you on track with your long-term vision? Revisiting your goals helps you stay flexible and allows you to make adjustments as needed.

If you're still uncertain about what success looks like for you, or you'd like to explore your goals further, check out the **What Does Success Mean to You? (The Quiz)** in the Appendix. It's designed to help you reflect on your unique vision of success and how you can take steps to achieve it.

Action Points

- Reflect on your artistic vision, including the themes, subjects, and messages that inspire your work.

- Set SMART goals—specific, measurable, achievable, relevant, and time-bound.
- Balance creative goals (exploring new techniques, creating innovative work) with financial goals (selling art, gaining representation, securing commissions).
- Break down long-term goals into manageable short-term steps to stay focused and motivated.
- Stay flexible and adjust your goals as your career evolves.
- Hold yourself accountable by documenting your goals, creating timelines, and regularly reviewing your progress.

3

Building a Sustainable Art Practice

C reating a sustainable art practice is about cultivating a balanced approach that ensures longevity in both your creative and business endeavors. For artists, this means finding a way to harmonize the demands of making art with the realities of earning a living, managing time, and nurturing emotional resilience. A sustainable practice allows you to continue evolving artistically, financially, and personally over the long term, without burnout or financial instability.

Sustainability is built on four interconnected pillars: creative sustainability, financial sustainability, emotional sustainability, and practical sustainability. Each plays a crucial role in helping you thrive as an artist while maintaining a balanced and fulfilling career.

Creative Sustainability: How to Keep Your Passion Burning Bright

At the heart of any artist's practice is the creative process. Creative sustainability ensures that your passion for art stays alive and that you have the freedom and flexibility to explore, experiment, and grow. Without this, even the most financially successful career can feel hollow or draining.

Here are ways to nurture your creative sustainability:

1. **Consistent Exploration and Experimentation**: Creativity thrives on exploration. Give yourself permission to experiment with new techniques, materials, and subjects regularly. Set aside time for play and risk-taking. These creative "side quests" often lead to breakthroughs or open new doors for your main body of work. Consider scheduling a "creative retreat" every few months where you focus solely on trying something new, without the pressure of creating a finished product.

2. **Establish Creative Rituals**: Rituals help create a mental transition into creative work. These can be as simple as starting your studio session with a meditation, lighting a candle, or listening to specific music. Such rituals build consistency and signal to your mind that it's time to focus on your art.

3. **Maintain a Creative Journal**: A journal can be a valuable tool for tracking creative ideas, inspirations, and reflections on your artistic journey. Use it to jot down thoughts, sketch, or reflect on your process. By

documenting your creative thoughts, you maintain an ongoing dialogue with your inner artist, which can help spark new ideas and keep your passion alive.

4. **Set Creative Goals**: While some artists find comfort in organic, unstructured creative processes, setting goals can provide direction and motivation. Creative goals might include finishing a certain number of pieces in a year, experimenting with a specific technique, completing a themed series, or planning a course or workshop. These goals help keep your work focused and ensure you're progressing over time.

5. **Stay Inspired by Surrounding Yourself with Art**: Constant inspiration is crucial for creative sustainability. Regularly visit galleries, museums, or art fairs to see the work of other artists. Seek out new art forms, read books on art history or technique, or attend online artist talks. The more exposed you are to different ideas and approaches, the more fuel you'll have to spark your own creativity.

6. **Combat Creative Burnout**: Every artist faces moments when creativity wanes. To avoid burnout, recognize when you need to step back. Engage in non-art-related activities like nature walks, hobbies, or socializing. These breaks refresh your mind, allowing creativity to return naturally.

Financial Sustainability: Building a Practice That Supports Your Life

Financial sustainability is one of the most important, yet challenging, aspects of maintaining a long-term art practice. Building a sustainable financial foundation means ensuring that you can generate enough income to support both your art practice and personal life. Achieving this balance can provide the stability needed to continue creating without constant financial stress.

Here are actionable steps for financial sustainability:

1. **Diversify Your Income Streams**: Solely relying on the sale of original artworks can make income unpredictable. Explore multiple income streams such as teaching workshops, offering online courses, selling limited edition prints, creating digital products, and licensing your work for merchandise or textiles. This diversification ensures that even if one revenue stream slows down, others can help fill the gap.

2. **Develop Passive Income Avenues**: In addition to selling original works, look for ways to earn passive income. This could include selling prints through print-on-demand services, licensing your art for products, or offering downloadable resources like eBooks or digital templates. Passive income allows you to generate earnings even when you're not actively creating new pieces.

3. **Pricing Your Art Effectively**: Setting the right price for your work is crucial for financial sustainability. Make sure your pricing covers not only the cost of

materials and time but also factors in your level of experience, the demand for your work, and your target market. Be confident in your pricing—don't undervalue your art out of fear. A well-calculated pricing strategy can help you maintain consistent sales and reinforce the perceived value of your work.

4. **Track Your Expenses and Revenue**: Keeping detailed records of your art-related income and expenses is essential. Track everything—from supplies to shipping costs to the time spent on each piece. Not only does this help you understand your actual profit margins, but it also allows you to adjust your prices, make smarter financial decisions, and prepare for tax time. Consider using accounting software designed for small businesses, like QuickBooks or Wave, to keep your finances organized.

5. **Financial Cushion for Stability**: Building a financial safety net is essential for a sustainable practice. Aim to save a portion of your income for unexpected expenses or slower sales periods. A financial cushion allows you to navigate tough times without compromising your creative practice.

6. **Plan for Taxes**: If you're a freelance artist, you'll likely be responsible for your own taxes. This means setting aside a portion of your income for taxes and keeping meticulous records. Consider working with a tax advisor who specializes in the art world to help you navigate deductions and ensure you're not caught off guard come tax season.

Emotional Sustainability: Protecting Your Mental and Emotional Well-Being

Sustaining an art practice is as much about mental health as it is about creativity or finances. Emotional resilience ensures that you can handle the inevitable challenges, including rejection, criticism, and financial uncertainty, without losing your drive.

Here's how to protect your emotional sustainability:

1. **Reframe Rejection and Criticism**: As an artist, you'll inevitably face rejection, whether it's from galleries, collectors, or competitions. Learn to reframe rejection as part of the process. Every "no" is an opportunity to learn and grow. It's important to develop a thick skin without losing your creative vulnerability. Surround yourself with a community that supports and uplifts you, helping you process feedback in a healthy way.

2. **Build a Supportive Network**: Having a strong support system of fellow artists, mentors, and friends can make all the difference. Regular check-ins, group critiques, and shared studio spaces can provide a sense of community and camaraderie. You don't have to navigate the challenges of an art career alone—lean on your network for encouragement and feedback.

3. **Establish Boundaries Between Work and Life**: Creative work can be emotionally consuming, and it's easy to blur the lines between your art and your personal life. Set boundaries to protect your emotional well-being, such as designated studio hours, regular

days off, or time spent on non-art-related activities. These boundaries help prevent burnout and give you the mental space to rejuvenate.

4. **Celebrate Small Wins**: It's easy to get discouraged when focusing on long-term goals, especially in the art world where success can feel elusive. Take time to acknowledge and celebrate the small wins—whether it's finishing a challenging piece, getting positive feedback, or selling a print. These moments of celebration remind you of the progress you're making.

5. **Practice Self-Care**: Creative work is deeply emotional, and it's important to take care of your mental and physical health. Engage in regular self-care activities like exercise, meditation, or journaling. Make sure you're getting enough rest and nourishing yourself with healthy meals. A healthy body and mind are crucial for maintaining creative flow.

Practical Sustainability: Building Systems for Long-Term Success

A sustainable art practice also requires practical strategies for managing your time, energy, and resources. These systems ensure that your art practice runs smoothly and that you have the infrastructure to support growth and success.

Here's how to establish practical sustainability:

1. **Create a Time Management System**: Time management is one of the biggest challenges for artists,

especially when balancing creative work with administrative tasks. Develop a system that allows you to manage both effectively. Consider using tools like Trello, Asana, or Google Calendar to schedule studio time, marketing efforts, and client communication.

2. **Set Up Automation for Administrative Tasks**: Automation can free up valuable time and reduce administrative burdens. Use tools like Later or Hootsuite to schedule social media posts, Mailchimp to automate your email newsletters, and FreshBooks to track invoices and expenses. Automating these tasks will allow you to focus more on your creative work.

3. **Create a Workspace That Inspires and Supports You**: A well-organized and inspiring studio space can significantly impact your productivity and creativity. Make sure your studio is organized, with tools and materials easily accessible. Consider creating distinct areas for different tasks—such as painting, sketching, and digital work—to help streamline your process.

4. **Track and Measure Your Progress**: Tracking your progress is essential for staying on course. Keep a log of completed works, exhibitions, and sales to evaluate what's working and where improvements can be made. This data can help you identify patterns, understand your strengths, and make informed decisions about future projects.

5. **Build and Maintain Relationships**: Cultivating long-term relationships with collectors, galleries, and collaborators is key to sustainability. Keep in touch

with past clients through newsletters, follow-up emails, or invitations to events. Building these connections creates a strong foundation for future opportunities.

6. **Regularly Review and Adjust**: Sustainability is not a static goal—it requires constant evaluation and adjustment. Set aside time every few months to review your goals, assess your financial health, and check in with your emotional well-being. Adjust your strategies as needed to ensure you're continuing to grow in a way that supports your long-term success.

Balancing Passion and Practicality

Building a sustainable art practice requires a careful balance between creativity, finances, emotional health, and practical systems. By nurturing all aspects of your career—artistic, financial, emotional, and organizational—you can create a foundation that allows you to thrive over the long term. Sustainability is about more than just survival—it's about building a practice that grows with you, evolves over time, and supports your passion for creating art.

4

Marketing Your Art

Marketing your art is about more than just getting your work in front of potential buyers—it's about creating meaningful connections, telling your story, and ensuring that your unique voice is heard in the often crowded and competitive art world. Successful art marketing requires a combination of strategy, persistence, and authenticity, allowing you to build a sustainable career while reaching the right audience.

The concept of marketing might seem daunting and foreign at first, particularly if you consider yourself more of a creator than a businessperson. But at its core, marketing is simply the process of communicating the value of your art to others.

Understanding Your Audience

Before you can market your art effectively, it's crucial to understand who you're marketing to. Your audience includes not only potential buyers but also fellow artists, gallery owners, curators, and even casual fans of art. Each of these groups can play a role in helping you grow your career, so understanding how to appeal to different segments of your audience is key.

Start by asking yourself some basic questions about your ideal audience. Who is most likely to connect with your work? Are they young collectors who might appreciate more experimental or abstract art? Or are they established collectors with a more traditional taste? Do they live in certain geographic areas, or are they connected to particular communities or industries?

Once you have a clear picture of your ideal audience, you can tailor your marketing efforts to speak directly to them. For instance, if your art focuses on urban landscapes, you might target collectors who live in cities or who have a strong connection to urban life. If you create art that explores themes of nature and sustainability, you might look for eco-conscious buyers or organizations that promote environmental causes.

One of the best ways to get to know your audience is by engaging with them directly. Whether through social media, email newsletters, or in-person events, take the time to have conversations, ask questions, and listen to what resonates with your followers. This ongoing dialogue will help you refine your messaging and create content that truly speaks to the people you want to reach.

Crafting Your Message

Once you understand your audience, the next step is to craft a message that resonates with them. The key to successful art marketing lies in storytelling. People don't just buy art because they like how it looks—they buy it because they feel a connection to the artist, the process, or the story behind the work.

When marketing your art, you should aim to tell the story of who you are as an artist, what inspires you, and why your work matters. This might include sharing the creative journey behind a particular piece, talking about the techniques you used, or explaining the emotions or experiences that shaped your art. These stories help create an emotional connection between you and your audience, making your work more memorable and impactful.

For example, instead of simply posting an image of a new painting on social media with a caption like "New work available," you might explain what inspired the piece. Perhaps it was a memory from your childhood or a trip that left a deep impression on you. Maybe you experimented with a new medium or technique that challenged you in new ways. These details invite your audience into your world and give them a reason to care about your art beyond its aesthetic appeal.

Your messaging should also reflect your values as an artist. If you're passionate about social issues, environmental sustainability, or any other cause, let that shine through in your marketing. Not only will this help differentiate you from other artists, but it will also attract like-minded people who are more likely to support your work.

Choosing the Right Platforms

Once you've crafted your message, the next step is deciding where to share it. In today's digital age, artists have more options than ever when it comes to marketing their work. While traditional marketing methods like gallery exhibitions and art fairs are still important, digital platforms offer an unparalleled opportunity to reach a global audience.

Let's explore some of the key platforms and how you can leverage them to market your art effectively.

Social Media

Social media is one of the most powerful tools at your disposal as an artist. Platforms like Instagram, Facebook, TikTok, and Pinterest allow you to showcase your work, connect with potential buyers, and build a community around your art. But simply posting images of your work isn't enough—you need to engage with your audience, share stories, and provide valuable content that keeps people coming back.

Instagram is particularly popular among artists because of its visual nature. Use Instagram not just to post finished pieces, but also to share behind-the-scenes content that gives your followers a glimpse into your creative process. You can post time-lapse videos of you working on a painting, share photos of your studio, or even go live to answer questions from your audience in real-time. By letting people see the person behind the art, you create a more personal connection with your followers.

On Facebook, you might consider joining or creating groups dedicated to art or specific themes that align with your work. Groups allow you to engage with a community of like-minded people, whether they're fellow artists, collectors, or simply fans of the arts. You can also use Facebook events to promote exhibitions, online sales, or even virtual studio tours.

TikTok, though known for its short-form videos, is becoming an increasingly popular platform for artists. You can create quick, engaging videos that show your process, share tips for other artists, or even participate in trending challenges to increase your visibility. The algorithm on TikTok is designed to help new users gain exposure, making it an excellent platform for building a following quickly.

Pinterest is another great platform for artists, especially those whose work lends itself to decor or design. Many users go to Pinterest for inspiration, making it a perfect place to showcase your art in context—whether that's a painting displayed in a living room or a sculpture in a garden.

Your Website

Your website is your digital home base. It's where potential buyers will go to learn more about you, browse your portfolio, and, ideally, make a purchase. Think of your website as a combination gallery and store—it should be easy to navigate, visually appealing, and full of information that helps visitors understand who you are and what you do.

Make sure your website includes high-quality images of your work, along with descriptions that provide context and insight into each piece. If you sell your work online, ensure that your e-commerce setup is user-friendly and secure. Include a section for your artist bio, an updated list of exhibitions or shows you're participating in, and links to your social media profiles.

SEO (search engine optimization) is also critical for your website. Use keywords that potential buyers might search for when looking for art. For example, if you create abstract landscapes, include terms like "abstract landscape painting" or "contemporary art for sale" in your website copy. This will help your site appear in search engine results, driving more organic traffic.

Email Marketing

While social media often steals the spotlight, email marketing is an incredibly powerful tool for artists. An email list allows you to communicate directly with people who are interested in your work, without having to compete with social media algorithms. Your emails land right in their inbox, ensuring that your message is seen by your audience.

To build your email list, you can add a signup form to your website, promote it on social media, and even collect email addresses at exhibitions or events. Once you have a list of subscribers, send regular newsletters to keep them engaged. These newsletters can include updates on new work, exclusive offers, behind-the-scenes content, and invitations to upcoming exhibitions or events.

Email marketing is also a great way to drive sales. For example, you could offer your subscribers early access to new collections or limited-time discounts on prints. By giving your email list special perks, you create a sense of exclusivity and reward those who are most invested in your career.

In-Person Marketing Opportunities

While digital marketing is essential, there's still immense value in in-person marketing opportunities. Participating in art fairs, exhibitions, and open studio events can help you build relationships with collectors, galleries, and fellow artists.

When marketing your art in person, presentation is key. Whether it's a solo exhibition at a gallery or a booth at an art fair, make sure your display is professional, cohesive, and reflective of your brand. Use signage, business cards, and other materials to ensure people can easily learn more about you and your work.

In-person events are also a great opportunity to tell your story. Take the time to talk to visitors about your process, inspiration, and the meaning behind your work. People are much more likely to buy art when they feel connected to the artist, so don't be shy about sharing your passion.

Another important aspect of in-person marketing is networking. The relationships you build with fellow artists, curators, and collectors can lead to future opportunities such as a gallery show, a commission, or a collaboration. Be sure to follow up with people after the event—send a thank-you email or message, connect on social media, and continue the conversation.

Pricing and Selling Your Work

One of the most challenging aspects of marketing your art is pricing it appropriately. Your pricing strategy needs to reflect the value of your work, your experience, and the market you're operating in. Pricing too low can undermine the perception of your work, while pricing too high can deter potential buyers. You need to find that "sweet spot."

When setting prices, consider factors like the cost of materials, the time spent creating the piece, your level of experience, and the prices of similar works by other artists in your niche. Be consistent in your pricing across different platforms—whether someone is buying from your website, at an exhibition, or through a gallery, the price should remain the same to maintain trust and transparency. Depending on how your work is sold, you will receive varying amounts from sales; however, the prices collectors see should be the same across all sales outlets.

Once you've set your prices, be confident in them. Don't undervalue your work just to make a sale. If someone is genuinely interested in your art, they will understand and respect the price you've set. However, offering limited-time discounts or special offers (such as free shipping or a bonus print with purchase) can be a great way to incentivize sales without devaluing your work.

Tracking and Adjusting Your Efforts

Marketing your art is an ongoing process, and it's important to track your efforts to see what's working and what isn't. Use tools like Google Analytics to monitor traffic to your website, social media insights to track engagement, and email marketing platforms to measure open and click-through rates.

By analyzing this data, you can identify patterns and make informed decisions about where to focus your marketing efforts. For example, if you notice that your Instagram posts about your creative process generate more engagement than posts about finished pieces, you can create more process-oriented content. If your email open rates are higher when you include a personal story, make storytelling a regular feature of your newsletters.

Don't be afraid to experiment with different approaches, platforms, and content types. Marketing is not a one-size-fits-all process, and what works for one artist might not work for another. The key is to remain flexible, track your results, and continually refine your strategy to better connect with your audience and grow your career.

Action Points

- Understand your audience and tailor your message to speak directly to their interests and values.
- Use storytelling to create an emotional connection with your audience. Share the inspiration, process, and meaning behind your work.
- Leverage social media platforms like Instagram,

Facebook, TikTok, and Pinterest to showcase your work and engage with your followers.

- Build and maintain a professional website that showcases your portfolio and includes e-commerce options for selling your art.
- Start an email list and send regular newsletters to keep your audience informed and engaged.
- Participate in in-person events like art fairs and exhibitions to build relationships and network with collectors and galleries.
- Set consistent prices for your work and be confident in your pricing strategy.
- Track your marketing efforts using analytics tools and adjust your strategy based on what resonates with your audience.

5

The Artist's Website

In today's digital-first world, an artist's website is one of the most powerful tools for building visibility, attracting collectors, and showcasing your work. It's not just an online gallery but a storefront, communication hub, and brand ambassador all rolled into one. A well-designed website allows you to take full control of your online presence, helping visitors connect with your art, learn your story, and potentially make a purchase—all without the constraints of social media algorithms.

Your website should not only showcase your art but also serve as a crucial tool for marketing, sales, and building lasting relationships with collectors and fans.

The Importance of a Professional Website

While social media, Etsy, or other online platforms are useful, they have limitations. A professional artist's website offers unparalleled control over how your work is presented. It's the central hub for all of your digital marketing efforts and allows you to:

- **Build Your Brand**: Your website is the best place to craft a cohesive, authentic brand. You control every aspect, from design and messaging to how visitors navigate through your site.
- **Create Direct Sales Opportunities**: A website can integrate a professional e-commerce platform where collectors can buy your work directly. No middleman, no platform fees (except for standard transaction costs), and full control over your pricing.
- **Provide a Centralized Portfolio**: Instead of scattering your work across various platforms, your website allows you to create a professional portfolio that potential buyers can access anytime.
- **Boost Credibility**: In a competitive art world, having a polished website signals that you are a serious professional. Galleries, curators, and collectors are more likely to work with artists who present themselves well online.

Creating a Website That Works: Step-by-Step

Now, let's break down each essential component of your artist website, providing practical advice and detailed strategies to maximize its effectiveness.

Homepage: The Virtual Front Door

Your homepage is your website's "first impression," and it needs to captivate visitors instantly. You have mere seconds to convince them to explore further.

- **Featured Work**: Your homepage should highlight a signature piece that encapsulates your style and artistic vision. This isn't just about beauty—it's about creating a strong connection with your audience. Use a high-quality image (minimum of 1500 pixels wide for sharpness across devices). If your work is three-dimensional, provide images from different angles to give a full sense of the piece.

  Pro Tip: If you work in series, you can rotate pieces from different collections on your homepage, offering a dynamic snapshot of your work.
- **Engaging Introductory Statement**: This is your elevator pitch in written form. Within two sentences, you need to convey who you are, what kind of work you create, and why it matters. Avoid jargon, but make it compelling. For example: "I'm a mixed-media

artist exploring the intersection of nature and emotion through vibrant, textural landscapes." Place this statement prominently on your homepage, either overlaid on the featured image or just below it.

- **Call to Action (CTA)**: Every homepage needs a clear and direct CTA. You want your visitors to know exactly what to do next—whether it's browsing your portfolio, purchasing artwork, or signing up for your newsletter. Use concise, action-oriented phrases like "Explore My Portfolio," "Shop Now," or "Get Exclusive Updates."

Pro Tip: Keep CTAs visually distinct by using contrasting colors or bold fonts to make them stand out from the rest of your homepage design.

About Page: Sharing Your Story

The About page is where visitors can get to know the artist behind the work. Potential buyers and galleries are often just as interested in your journey as they are in the art itself. This page should humanize you, making visitors feel personally connected to your creative process.

- **Biography**: Write a concise yet engaging narrative that outlines your artistic journey. Highlight key moments such as when you discovered your passion, formal education (if applicable), and important shifts in your career. Keep the tone conversational but professional —your goal is to be relatable without losing credibility.

For example, "Growing up surrounded by the forests of the Pacific Northwest, I was drawn to capturing the raw beauty of nature in my work. After studying environmental science, I transitioned into full-time painting to explore these themes artistically."

Pro Tip: If you work with recurring themes (e.g., nature, emotions, societal commentary), mention them in your biography. This helps visitors understand the driving force behind your work.

- **Artist Statement**: Dive into the meaning behind your work. While your biography touches on your journey, the artist statement should explain the themes, techniques, and materials that define your art. Avoid overly complex language—art collectors want insight but not an academic lecture. For instance, "In my recent series, I've focused on the tension between urban life and nature, using rough textures and organic materials to create a dialogue between the built and natural environments."

- **Process Description**: Many art buyers are fascinated by how a piece is made. Include a short section about your process—what materials you use, any special techniques, and how a piece evolves from idea to completion.

- **Headshot**: A professional photograph of you, preferably in your studio or with your work, adds a personal touch to the About page. It helps visitors put a face to the art and makes you more relatable.

Portfolio: Displaying Your Work

Your portfolio is the heart of your website. This is where visitors can explore your work in-depth, and for many, it's the deciding factor in whether or not they make a purchase or inquire about your art.

- **Organized Layout**: Structure your portfolio so that it's easy to navigate. Divide your works into categories or series. For instance, if you have a collection of abstract paintings and another of landscape photography, make sure each category is clearly labeled. This helps potential buyers find exactly what they're looking for without having to sift through unrelated pieces.
- **Multiple Images**: For each artwork, provide several images: full views, close-ups of textures or details, and shots of the work in a setting (e.g., hung on a wall or displayed in a room). This gives visitors a fuller understanding of the work's dimensions, texture, and scale.

  Pro Tip: Use professional photography to capture your work in the best light. High-quality images are critical —blurry or poorly lit photos can make even great art seem unappealing.
- **Descriptions**: Don't just list the title and dimensions —provide context. Each piece should have a brief but informative description, explaining the inspiration behind it, the materials used, and any special techniques. This adds depth and helps potential buyers or collectors connect with the artwork on a more emotional level.

- **Zoom Functionality**: Allow visitors to zoom in on images to see fine details. This is especially important for online buyers who can't view the work in person. Most website builders offer this feature as part of their portfolio functionality.

E-Commerce: Selling Your Art

One of the most powerful benefits of an artist's website is the ability to sell your work directly to collectors. If you plan to handle sales on your website, integrating an e-commerce platform is essential.

- **Choosing a Platform**: Website builders like Squarespace, Wix, and Shopify all have built-in e-commerce capabilities. Select a platform that provides secure payment processing, supports multiple currencies (if needed), and has options for shipping calculation and tax collection.

  Pro Tip: If you sell limited editions, make sure your site tracks how many remain and displays that information to potential buyers. Scarcity often drives urgency in art purchases.
- **Product Pages**: Each piece of art you're selling should have its own product page. Include the following information:

  ○ Title and year created

- Materials and dimensions
- Price
- Shipping details
- Availability (e.g., limited edition, one-of-a-kind)
- A "Buy Now" or "Add to Cart" button for easy purchasing

Pro Tip: Use a clean, simple checkout process. The fewer clicks and fields to fill out, the better. Complicated checkouts can lead to abandoned carts.

Contact Page: Encouraging Engagement

The Contact page may seem straightforward, but it's an essential part of converting interest into action. Whether it's inquiries about purchasing art, setting up a studio visit, or simply getting in touch for a collaboration, make this process as easy as possible.

- **Email and Contact Form**: Display your email address prominently, but also include a contact form for convenience. The form should be simple, asking only for essential information (name, email, and message).

Pro Tip: Use CAPTCHA or other security measures to avoid spam from automated bots.

- **Social Media Links**: Link to your social media profiles, encouraging visitors to follow you for more updates and behind-the-scenes content. This helps keep your audience engaged beyond their visit to your website.

- **Studio Visits and Commissions**: If you offer studio visits or commissions, explain the process briefly and invite visitors to inquire. For example, "I welcome studio visits by appointment. Please get in touch via email to schedule a time."

SEO and Analytics: Making Your Website Visible

Building a beautiful website is only the first step—you also need people to find it. This is where SEO (Search Engine Optimization) and analytics come in.

- **SEO**: Use keywords strategically throughout your site, especially in headings, image descriptions, and your About page. Think about what collectors or curators might search for—terms like "contemporary abstract artist," "art for sale online," or "landscape painting in New York." Integrating these phrases naturally into your text can help your site rank higher on Google.

  Pro Tip: Update your website regularly with new content (like blog posts or portfolio updates) to keep it relevant and improve SEO rankings.
- **Analytics**: Use Google Analytics or a built-in tool from your website platform to track visitor behavior. Pay attention to which pages get the most traffic, how

long visitors stay on your site, and where they drop off. This information can help you refine your website over time to maximize engagement and sales.

Blogging: Keeping Your Audience Engaged

Maintaining a blog is a fantastic way to keep your website dynamic and offer more insight into your work. Blog posts give you a chance to dive deeper into your creative process, announce new collections, or share your thoughts on trends in the art world.

- **Process Stories**: Write about the creation of specific pieces or collections. Include photos of the work in progress, sketches, and even mistakes along the way. Buyers love to feel involved in the creative journey.
- **Announcements**: Use your blog to announce upcoming exhibitions, events, or special projects. This helps drive traffic back to your website whenever you have something new to share.

Action Points

- **Choose a Website Builder**: Select a platform that fits your design needs and offers integrated e-commerce features.
- **Build a Compelling Homepage**: Use high-quality images and a clear call to action to draw visitors in.
- **Create an Engaging About Page**: Share your story in

a professional yet personal way to build a connection with your audience.

- **Organize Your Portfolio**: Structure your artwork into clear categories and provide detailed descriptions.
- **Implement E-Commerce**: Set up a seamless sales process that includes product pages, secure payment options, and shipping details.
- **Focus on SEO**: Use relevant keywords throughout your site to improve visibility on search engines.
- **Maintain a Blog**: Keep your audience engaged by regularly updating your blog with insights, stories, and announcements.
- **Analyze Performance**: Use analytics to track your website's performance and adjust your strategy as needed.

6

Harnessing the Power of Social Media

S ocial media has become one of the most important tools in an artist's marketing toolbox. It allows you to reach a vast and diverse audience, showcase your work to potential collectors, and build a personal connection with your fans. Gone are the days when artists could rely solely on gallery representation or word of mouth to find success. Today, social media is essential for building visibility, establishing your brand, and connecting with your audience in real time. Social media is one of the most effective ways to grow your art career in today's digital world, and with the right strategies in place, you can leverage these platforms to your full advantage.

The Power of Social Media for Artists

Social media has revolutionized the art world by removing traditional barriers between artists and their audiences. You no longer need to wait for a gallery show or exhibition to showcase your work; with the click of a button, you can share your latest pieces with thousands of followers. Social media enables you to build an intimate connection with your audience by sharing behind-the-scenes content, your creative process, and personal stories that resonate with them. By fostering this type of engagement, you deepen the connection between you and your audience, encouraging long-term relationships and potential sales.

One of the key advantages of social media is its visual nature, making it an ideal medium for artists. Platforms like Instagram, Pinterest, and TikTok are heavily image- and video-based, allowing artists to showcase their work in high definition and with dynamic content like time-lapse videos or studio tours. Furthermore, social media offers a global stage, where artists from anywhere in the world can connect with collectors, galleries, and fellow creatives—all without leaving their studio.

Choosing the Right Platform

Not all social media platforms are created equal, and it's important to choose the right one(s) for your needs. Each platform has its own strengths, demographics, and best practices, and not every platform will suit every artist's style or audience. Below is an expanded look at the most popular platforms for artists, complete with deeper insights and examples to guide your approach.

Instagram

Instagram is the most popular platform for artists, thanks to its visual-first format. It allows you to share high-quality images and videos of your work, engage with followers through Stories, and sell directly via the platform's e-commerce features.

- **What works on Instagram**: High-quality images, short videos (Reels), and behind-the-scenes content. For example, artist *Yayoi Kusama* uses Instagram to post time-lapse videos of her painting process and behind-the-scenes looks at her exhibitions. Posting a time-lapse of your painting process or showing step-by-step progress updates helps followers connect with your work on a deeper level.
- **Engagement strategies**: Use Instagram Stories to keep followers engaged with polls, Q&As, and sneak peeks of upcoming projects. Reels are ideal for showing quick snippets of your creative process or promoting new pieces. Engaging with other artists, galleries, and collectors through comments and direct messages can also build relationships and grow your following.
- **Hashtags**: Hashtags are critical for visibility on Instagram. While it's tempting to use the maximum 30 hashtags per post, focus on quality over quantity. Research niche-specific hashtags that cater to your style

and audience. For example, a landscape painter might use hashtags like #landscapepainting or #natureart, while an abstract artist could use #abstractexpressionism or #modernart. Always include a mix of broad and specific hashtags to reach both wide and targeted audiences.

Advanced Tip: Try leveraging Instagram's *Collaborate* feature by working with other artists or influencers on joint projects. For instance, you could do a collaboration with a fashion designer and show how your artwork influences their design, or work with an influencer who promotes your work by featuring it in their home.

Facebook

Though Facebook has become less popular among younger audiences, it still boasts a massive user base and can be particularly effective for targeting older collectors or art buyers. Its powerful ad system and the ability to create groups and events make it a strong platform for artists looking to engage with niche communities.

- **What works on Facebook**: Long-form posts, event promotions, and direct engagement with followers. Facebook also allows for in-depth storytelling—an artist can post about the inspirations behind a particular piece or share how they overcame creative blocks in a recent project. The visual artist *Carrie Mae Weems* regularly uses Facebook to promote her exhibitions and share thoughtful insights about her work, creating deeper engagement with her followers.

- **Engagement strategies**: Join and actively participate in Facebook Groups related to art, such as those for art collectors or local artist communities. These groups provide valuable networking opportunities, letting you connect with collectors or galleries in your niche. Some artists also create their own groups, which serve as communities for collectors and fans to engage with their work and each other.

- **Facebook Ads**: If you have a budget for paid promotion, Facebook Ads offer robust targeting options, allowing you to reach specific audiences based on interests, demographics, and behaviors. For instance, if you create contemporary abstract art, you can target art collectors interested in abstract art or buyers in specific regions. You can also retarget people who have visited your website but haven't yet made a purchase.

TikTok

TikTok is one of the fastest-growing social media platforms, especially among younger audiences. Its short-form video format offers a fun and creative way for artists to showcase their work, their process, and their personality.

- **What works on TikTok**: Short, engaging videos that capture attention quickly. For artists, this could mean time-lapse videos of your painting process, step-by-step tutorials, or creatively showing off a finished piece. *Takashi Murakami* has successfully used TikTok to show how he merges pop culture with fine art, creating dynamic videos that capture his process.

- **Engagement strategies**: TikTok's algorithm rewards content that is shared and commented on, so encouraging your followers to interact with your videos is key. You can run challenges or "duets," where users respond to your video with their own. For example, you could create a #paintwithme challenge and invite other artists or fans to show their process alongside yours.
- **Hashtags**: Like Instagram, hashtags are critical on TikTok. Use art-related hashtags like #ArtTok or #artistsonTikTok, but also tap into trending or viral hashtags to increase the chance of your content reaching a wider audience.

Advanced Tip: TikTok allows for spontaneous, creative engagement. Try showing off less-polished, in-progress work or humorous studio moments. Viewers often appreciate the raw, unfiltered aspects of the creative process, which helps build a more authentic connection.

LinkedIn

LinkedIn is often overlooked by artists, but it can be a valuable platform for connecting with galleries, art consultants, corporate buyers, and other professionals in the art world.

LinkedIn is the place to position yourself as both a creative and a business professional.

- **What works on LinkedIn**: Posting professional articles about your work, sharing exhibition announcements, and discussing industry trends or the business side of being an artist. You can showcase your professionalism by writing posts about how you manage commissions, how you structure pricing, or how you run the business side of your art practice.
- **Engagement strategies**: LinkedIn is more formal than other platforms, so focus on professional engagement. Publish articles, engage with other professionals in the art world, and showcase your skills and achievements. Participating in LinkedIn Groups related to the art world is also a great way to network and find new opportunities.
- **Networking**: LinkedIn is particularly valuable for artists seeking to connect with B2B (business-to-business) opportunities. For example, if you want to work with interior designers or art consultants for corporate collections, LinkedIn provides a platform to engage with those professionals directly.

Advanced Tip: Showcase your expertise by offering insights into your process through long-form articles. For example, write an article on the evolution of your art style, discussing major influences or techniques you've mastered over the years. This demonstrates thought leadership and positions you as an expert in your field.

Pinterest

Pinterest is a powerful platform for artists, particularly those whose work appeals to designers, decorators, or those interested in DIY projects. Many people use Pinterest for inspiration when decorating their homes or offices, and they're often looking for artwork to complement their spaces.

- **What works on Pinterest**: High-quality, vertically oriented images of your art with links to your website or online store. Pinterest is also great for sharing curated boards of your work, inspiration, and mood boards that reflect your style and process. This platform works especially well for artists who create decorative, contemporary, or design-focused work.
- **Engagement strategies**: Regularly upload new pins featuring your latest works, as well as any blog posts, articles, or videos you've created about your art. Engage with other users by repinning their content and commenting on their boards. Consider creating a board that outlines your artistic process, from inspiration to completed work.
- **Keywords**: Pinterest functions more like a search engine than a social media platform, so make sure you use strong keywords in your pin descriptions. For instance, if you're a portrait artist, keywords like "commissioned

portrait painting" or "custom family portraits" can help you attract the right audience.

Growing Your Audience

Once you've chosen your platform(s), the next step is to grow your audience. Building a following takes time, but with the right strategies, you can attract engaged followers who are genuinely interested in your work.

Consistent Posting

Consistency is key when it comes to social media. Posting regularly helps keep your followers engaged and makes it more likely that your content will be shown in their feeds. Create a posting schedule that works for you—whether that's daily, three times a week, or even once a week—and stick to it. Tools like Hootsuite or Later can help you schedule posts in advance, so you don't have to manually post each day.

Example: Consider how *Banksy* uses his social media accounts. He rarely posts, but when he does, it creates a frenzy of engagement because his posts are deliberate and thought-provoking. While most artists need more frequent posts, this illustrates the power of strategic, timely content.

Engaging Content

Posting regularly is important, but the quality of your content matters even more. Your audience is most likely to engage with content that resonates with them on a personal or emotional level. Think about what stories you can tell through your art:

- **Behind-the-scenes**: Show what goes into creating your work, from sketching ideas to mixing paints to putting on the final touches. Followers love seeing the raw, unpolished moments of creativity.
- **Your process**: Share your techniques and explain why you choose certain materials or methods. *Shepard Fairey* often explains the inspiration behind his iconic street art in social media posts, which helps connect his audience to his creative vision.
- **Inspiration**: Talk about what inspires you, whether it's nature, architecture, personal experiences, or something else. *Frida Kahlo's* Instagram account frequently shares quotes from her writings that align with her artistic spirit, offering followers a personal connection to her work.

Interact with Followers

Social media is a two-way street. Don't just post your work and move on—take the time to engage with your followers. Respond to comments, ask questions in your posts, and encourage followers to share their thoughts. The more you interact with your audience, the more connected they'll feel to you and your art.

Example: Consider hosting an Instagram Live Q&A

where you answer questions from your followers about your creative process, inspiration, or upcoming projects. This kind of personal interaction fosters stronger relationships with your audience.

Collaborate with Other Artists and Influencers

Collaboration is a powerful way to grow your following and expand your reach. Consider working with other artists or influencers to create joint projects, host giveaways, or simply cross-promote each other's work. For example, you could collaborate on a themed series with another artist or work with a popular art blogger to feature your work on their platform.

Influencers—especially those with large followings on Instagram, TikTok, or YouTube—can be particularly valuable in helping you reach new audiences. A single post or shout-out from the right influencer can introduce your work to thousands of new potential followers and collectors.

Selling Through Social Media

While social media is great for building your audience, it's also a powerful sales tool. More and more artists are using platforms like Instagram, Facebook, and even Pinterest to sell their work directly to collectors, bypassing traditional galleries and art fairs.

Instagram Shopping

Instagram's shopping feature allows you to sell directly through the platform. You can tag products (in this case, your art) in your posts and Stories, making it easy for followers to click and purchase. This is especially useful for selling prints, merchandise, or smaller works that are priced for online buyers.

Setting up Instagram Shopping: To use Instagram Shopping, you'll need to set up a shop through Facebook (since Instagram is owned by Facebook) and connect it to your Instagram account. You'll also need to ensure that your website has an e-commerce platform that supports product listings.

Best practices: Use high-quality images to showcase your work and make sure your product descriptions are clear and compelling. You can also use Instagram Stories to highlight new products, sales, or limited-time offers.

Direct Sales Through DMs

Many artists sell directly through direct messages (DMs) on platforms like Instagram and Facebook. If a follower is interested in purchasing a piece, they can message you directly to inquire about prices, shipping, and other details. Make sure to clearly communicate your process for selling through DMs, and don't be afraid to reach out to followers who express interest in your work.

Price transparency: While some artists prefer to keep prices private and only share them with interested buyers via DM, others have found success by listing prices upfront. This can streamline the sales process and make it easier for potential buyers to make a decision.

Measuring Success

It's important to track the effectiveness of your social media efforts to see what's working and where you can improve. Most platforms offer insights or analytics that show you how your posts are performing. Below are the key metrics to track.

- **Engagement rate**: This measures how many people are liking, commenting, or sharing your posts. A high engagement rate means your audience is interacting with your content, which is a good sign that they're invested in your work.
- **Follower growth**: Track how your follower count grows over time. While it's not the only measure of success, a steadily growing following indicates that your content is reaching new people and resonating with your audience.
- **Website traffic**: Use tools like Google Analytics to see how much traffic your social media posts are driving to your website or online store. If a post about a new collection leads to a spike in website visits, that's a good indicator that your social media strategy is working.

Adjusting Your Strategy

Social media is constantly evolving, and what works today might not work tomorrow. Don't be afraid to experiment with different types of content, posting schedules, or platforms. If something isn't working, adjust your strategy based on the data you collect.

For example, if you notice that your Instagram posts are getting more engagement than your Facebook posts, consider shifting more of your focus to Instagram. Or if videos are consistently outperforming photos, start incorporating more video content into your strategy.

Action Points

- Choose the right platform(s) for your art and audience.
- Post consistently and create a schedule that works for you.
- Engage with your followers regularly to build strong connections.
- Use relevant hashtags and keywords to increase visibility.
- Leverage platforms like Instagram Shopping and LinkedIn to sell your work.
- Track key metrics like engagement rates and follower growth to assess your social media strategy.
- Adjust your strategy based on analytics and insights.

7

Content Marketing for Artists: Blogging and Email Newsletters

In today's fast-paced digital landscape, artists must do more than just create and showcase their work. To build meaningful, lasting relationships with collectors, fans, and followers, artists need effective content marketing strategies. Two of the most powerful tools in this area are blogging and email newsletters. While social media platforms come and go, blogs and newsletters offer artists a way to communicate directly with their audience in a more intimate, controlled, and lasting manner. By using blogging and email newsletters as part of your content marketing strategy, you'll not only engage with your audience on a deeper level but also build lasting relationships that will grow your art business over time.

Blogging for Artists: Telling Your Story, Building Connections

Blogging offers artists a personal and versatile platform to engage deeply with their audience. It allows you to tell your story in your own words, share the inspiration behind your work, and provide insights into your creative process. While social media posts may be fleeting and easily overlooked, a blog serves as a more permanent space where your content can live and continue to drive traffic to your website for years to come.

Your blog can be more than just a showcase of your art. It's an opportunity to position yourself as a thought leader, invite people into your creative world, and forge connections that go beyond the transactional. A well-maintained blog creates long-term relationships that often lead to increased visibility, loyal fans, and sales.

The Benefits of Blogging for Artists

- **Personal Connection**: A blog provides a unique platform to connect with your audience on a deeper level. It's where you can share your creative process, inspirations, challenges, and successes. Readers who feel invested in your journey as an artist are more likely to become repeat buyers and passionate advocates of your work.

- **SEO and Online Visibility**: Search engine optimization (SEO) is one of the key benefits of having a blog. Google and other search engines favor websites that consistently publish fresh, high-quality content. By regularly updating your blog with relevant content (like new artwork, exhibitions, or personal insights into the art world), you can significantly improve your search rankings and attract new visitors to your website.

- **Building Authority and Trust**: By sharing your knowledge and experiences, you position yourself as an expert in your field. You can write posts about your techniques, insights into the art market, or even trends you're noticing. Establishing authority in your niche helps attract a loyal following who will not only purchase your art but also recommend you to others.

- **Evergreen Content**: One of the best features of a blog is that the content remains relevant long after it's published. Evergreen posts—those that remain useful and engaging over time—can continue to draw traffic to your site for months or even years. For example, an article titled "How to Care for Your Fine Art Collection" will stay relevant to art collectors indefinitely, continually driving visitors to your website.

What Should You Blog About?

As an artist, you might wonder what kinds of topics are best suited for a blog. Fortunately, you have a wealth of potential subjects to draw from that will resonate with your audience.

- **Your Creative Process**: Share behind-the-scenes details about how you create your work. This could include time-lapse videos, step-by-step breakdowns, or photos of your work in progress. People love to see the process behind the finished product, and it helps them feel more connected to the work.
- **Inspiration and Influences**: Talk about the things that inspire your art. Whether it's travel, nature, music, or other artists, sharing what drives your creativity gives your audience a deeper understanding of your work. This can create an emotional connection with your readers, which is key to converting them into buyers.
- **Upcoming Projects or Exhibitions**: Keep your audience updated on what's coming next. Share sneak peeks of new series or talk about upcoming exhibitions, art fairs, or gallery shows you'll be participating in. This not only keeps your readers engaged but also builds anticipation and encourages them to attend your events or buy your work when it's released.
- **Art Tutorials and Tips**: Sharing your expertise by offering tutorials or tips on art techniques can broaden your audience. Other artists (or aspiring artists) may find your insights valuable and start following your

blog for inspiration and advice. For example, you could create a post like "5 Essential Tips for Mixing Colors in Acrylic Painting."

- **Art World Insights**: Share your thoughts on trends, exhibitions you've visited, or news within the art world. By positioning yourself as someone with a finger on the pulse of the industry, you can attract readers who are interested not just in your art but also in your perspective on the art world.

- **Personal Stories**: Telling personal stories about your journey as an artist—challenges you've faced, breakthroughs you've experienced, or key moments that shaped your career—helps humanize you to your audience. Collectors often buy art because they connect with the artist, not just the work. By sharing more about yourself, you invite people to become part of your journey.

Blogging to Drive Sales

Your blog can be more than just a tool for engagement—it can also drive sales. By strategically using your blog to promote your art, you can create a natural sales funnel that guides your readers from being casual browsers to paying customers.

- **Share New Work**: Use your blog to announce new pieces or collections. Include high-quality images of the work, along with stories about the inspiration behind each piece. You can subtly include a call-to-action, such as "This piece is available for purchase here" with a link to your online store.

- **Lead Magnets**: Offer valuable content in exchange for an email sign-up. For example, you could offer a downloadable guide, exclusive behind-the-scenes videos, or a discount on your next print sale. By capturing email addresses through your blog, you can nurture these leads with your email newsletter (which we'll discuss next) and ultimately drive sales.
- **Highlight Art for Sale**: When discussing specific pieces or collections, be sure to mention that they are available for purchase. Include links to your shop or contact form, and make it easy for people to inquire about pricing or availability.

Tips for a Successful Blog

- **Consistency**: Blogging only works if you're consistent. Set a realistic schedule—whether that's once a week or once a month—and stick to it. Consistency helps build trust with your audience and keeps them coming back for more.
- **Use Visuals**: As a visual artist, your blog should showcase your work in the best light. Include high-quality images, videos, and even sketches to make your blog visually engaging. This not only enhances the reader's experience but also keeps them on your site longer.
- **Pay Attention to SEO**: Use keywords that your audience might search for, like "contemporary abstract

painting," "affordable fine art," or "how to care for acrylic paintings." Include these naturally in your titles, headings, and body text to help search engines find your content.

- **Engage with Your Readers**: Encourage your readers to leave comments, ask questions, or share their thoughts on your posts. Responding to comments shows that you value their input and helps build a community around your art.

Email Newsletters: Your Direct Line to Collectors and Fans

While social media is great for reaching a wide audience, email newsletters allow you to communicate directly with those who are truly invested in your work. Unlike social media algorithms, which can limit the reach of your posts, emails land straight in your subscribers' inboxes. A well-crafted email newsletter helps you build deeper relationships with your audience, stay top of mind, and, most importantly, drive sales.

Why You Need an Email List

An email list is one of the most valuable tools in an artist's marketing toolkit. Unlike social media followers, email subscribers have opted in to hear from you, which means they're already interested in your work and more likely to engage with your content. Here are three key reasons why building an email list is essential for artists:

- **Direct Communication**: With an email list, you have a direct line to your audience. This allows you to communicate more personally and consistently with your most engaged followers.
- **Sales and Promotion**: Email is an excellent tool for promoting new work, offering exclusive discounts, or giving subscribers early access to your latest collections. You can also send invitations to exhibitions, studio tours, or other events.
- **Building Relationships**: Regular email communication helps keep your audience connected to your art. By sharing updates, stories, and exclusive content, you deepen your relationship with collectors and fans, encouraging them to support your work over time.

Setting Up Your Newsletter

Creating an effective email newsletter involves more than just sending an occasional update. To maximize its impact, you'll need to design your newsletter carefully and craft content that resonates with your audience.

- **Design and Branding**: The look and feel of your newsletter should reflect your artistic brand. Use colors, fonts, and images that are consistent with your website and social media profiles. Keep the layout simple and visually appealing, ensuring that your artwork takes center stage.

- **Personalized Content**: Your emails should feel personal and engaging. Address your subscribers by their first names, if possible, and write in a friendly, conversational tone. Share stories about your creative process, upcoming projects, and new work.

- **Clear Call to Action**: Each newsletter should have a clear purpose, whether it's driving traffic to your website, promoting a new collection, or encouraging subscribers to follow you on social media. Include a strong call-to-action (CTA) such as "Shop My Latest Collection" or "RSVP for My Upcoming Exhibition."

- **Exclusive Content**: Reward your email subscribers by offering them something exclusive, such as early access to new work, special discounts, or behind-the-scenes content that isn't available elsewhere.

- **Mobile Optimization**: Many people will open your emails on their phones, so make sure your newsletter is mobile-friendly. This means using a simple layout, keeping images small enough to load quickly, and ensuring that buttons and links are easy to tap on a mobile screen.

Content Ideas for Email Newsletters

Like blog posts, your newsletters should provide value to your subscribers. Here are some content ideas that will keep your audience engaged and excited about your work:

- **Showcase New Work**: Give subscribers an exclusive look at your latest pieces before they're made public. Include high-quality images and tell the story behind each piece.
- **Studio Updates**: Share what's happening in your studio—whether it's a new technique you're experimenting with, materials you're trying, or behind-the-scenes shots of work in progress.
- **Personal Insights**: Let your subscribers in on your creative journey by sharing personal stories, thoughts on the art world, or reflections on your work. This builds a deeper connection with your audience.
- **Event Invitations**: Use your newsletter to promote upcoming exhibitions, art fairs, or virtual events. Make it easy for subscribers to RSVP or find more information.
- **Exclusive Offers**: Reward your most loyal followers by offering them exclusive discounts or promotions that aren't available to the public.

Building Your Email List

Growing your email list takes time, but the more subscribers you have, the more effective your newsletters will be. Here are a few strategies for building your list:

- **Add Sign-Up Forms to Your Website**: Place sign-up forms on key pages of your website, including your homepage, blog, and portfolio pages. Consider offering a lead magnet—such as a free downloadable print or a discount on your work—to encourage visitors to subscribe.

- **Promote Your Newsletter on Social Media**: Let your followers know that they can get exclusive updates and offers by signing up for your newsletter. Include a link to your sign-up form in your social media bios and regularly remind your followers to subscribe.

- **Collect Emails at Events**: When you attend art fairs, exhibitions, or open studios, ask visitors if they'd like to join your mailing list. You can provide a physical sign-up sheet or direct them to an online form on your website.

Automation and Analytics

Email marketing platforms like Mailchimp, ConvertKit, or MailerLite offer automation features that save you time and help ensure consistency. For example, you can set up an automated welcome series that introduces new subscribers to your work, or a series of emails promoting a new collection.

Tracking the performance of your emails is essential for improving your strategy. Pay attention to key metrics like:

- **Open Rates**: How many people opened your email? This can give you insights into how effective your subject lines are.

- **Click-Through Rates**: How many people clicked on

links in your email? This shows how engaged your audience is with the content you're sharing.

- **Unsubscribe Rates**: How many people are opting out of your emails? If this number is high, it may be a sign that you need to refine your content or send emails less frequently.

Action Points

- **Start a blog on your website** and update it regularly with behind-the-scenes content, personal stories, and new work.
- **Focus on SEO** to ensure your blog posts are discoverable by people searching for topics related to your art.
- **Set up an email marketing platform** like Mailchimp or ConvertKit and design a visually appealing, branded newsletter.
- **Offer lead magnets** (exclusive content or discounts) to grow your email list.
- **Promote your newsletter** across your website and social media channels.
- **Send regular newsletters** with engaging content that highlights new work, upcoming events, and personal insights.
- **Track performance metrics** like open rates, click-through rates, and engagement to optimize your content.

8

Exhibitions and Art Shows

Participating in exhibitions and art shows is one of the most exciting and rewarding experiences for an artist. Exhibitions allow you to showcase your work, interact with the public, build relationships with galleries, collectors, and fellow artists, and generate sales. Whether you're organizing a solo show, joining a group exhibition, or participating in an art fair, these events can be critical turning points in your career. They provide an opportunity to grow your audience, gain exposure, and elevate your profile in the art world.

Preparing for Your Exhibition

When preparing for an exhibition, it's important to be organized and strategic. Start planning well in advance, especially if it's your first show or if you're working with a gallery. The preparation phase typically involves selecting your work, curating the layout, setting prices, and handling logistics like framing, transportation, and installation.

Curating Your Work

Curating an exhibition requires more than simply selecting your favorite pieces. You need to think about how the works relate to each other and how the audience will experience them. This is particularly important for solo exhibitions where your work will be the sole focus. For group shows, you'll want to consider how your work fits into the overall theme of the exhibition.

For a **solo exhibition**, think about creating a cohesive body of work that tells a story or explores a particular theme. The pieces should feel like they belong together while also showcasing different aspects of your artistic range. If you have a large body of work, you may need to select only a portion of it to create a tighter, more impactful show.

For **group exhibitions**, consider how your pieces will interact with the work of other artists. Group shows often have a central theme, and your goal is to make sure your work complements the overall exhibition while still standing out. In a group setting, you may only have space for a few pieces, so choose those that best represent your artistic vision and are likely to attract attention.

Curating Visual Flow: Whether it's a solo or group exhibition, think about how people will move through the space. Start with a strong, eye-catching piece at the entrance to draw visitors in. Arrange works in a way that encourages viewers to linger and engage. Consider mixing large statement pieces with smaller, more intimate works to create visual variety and rhythm throughout the exhibition.

Examples of Successful Curated Exhibitions: Look at famous exhibitions for inspiration. For example, "The Forever Now: Contemporary Painting in an Atemporal World" at MoMA (2014-2015) brought together diverse contemporary painters under the theme of "atemporality," yet the exhibition layout created a seamless experience for visitors to engage with each work individually and as part of a whole. Studying such examples can help you understand how the arrangement of artworks can enhance the viewer's experience.

Framing and Presentation

Presentation matters, and it's essential that your work is displayed in the best possible way. The framing, lighting, and placement of your work can affect how it's perceived by the audience and potential buyers.

Framing Considerations: Choose frames that complement your artwork without overshadowing it. For example, minimalist frames work well for contemporary art, while more ornate frames may suit traditional or classical pieces. If your work is large, frameless canvas stretching can create a bold, modern look. Always ensure that the frames are high-quality and professionally fitted—cheap frames can detract from even the best artwork.

For works on paper, consider adding matting to create a clean, professional presentation. Matting also helps protect the artwork by keeping it from directly touching the glass. For sculptures, choose pedestals or stands that are sturdy and proportional to the size and weight of the piece.

Lighting: Lighting is a critical part of the exhibition experience. Well-placed lighting can enhance the colors and textures of your work, while poor lighting can dull its impact. If you have control over the lighting, work with the gallery or venue to ensure that each piece is properly illuminated. Spotlights are ideal for highlighting specific works, while ambient lighting can help set the overall mood.

In some cases, it may be necessary to add directional lighting to bring out details in sculptures or textured paintings. Be mindful of glare—especially on pieces behind glass—by positioning lights at angles that reduce reflections.

Pricing Your Work

Setting the right price for your art is one of the most important decisions you'll make. Price too high, and you risk alienating potential buyers; price too low, and you may undervalue your work and diminish your professional standing.

Pricing Strategies: Start by researching the market. Look at the prices of artists at a similar career stage or those working in a similar medium. This will give you a rough idea of where your pricing should start.

For solo exhibitions, consider setting prices at various levels to appeal to a range of buyers. For example, you might offer smaller works or prints at lower price points while setting higher prices for large or more intricate pieces. This allows people with different budgets to engage with your work.

For group exhibitions, it's important to remain competitive but not undersell your work. Align your pricing with the other artists in the show while maintaining consistency with your broader pricing strategy.

Another approach is the **square inch method**, where you calculate the price of a piece based on its size. For example, if you price your work at $2 per square inch, an 18x24-inch painting would be priced at $864. Adjust the rate per square inch based on your experience, the medium, and the complexity of the work. While this method provides a clear starting point, be sure to adjust for factors like rarity, demand, and time invested in each piece.

Promoting Your Exhibition

Promotion is key to ensuring a successful exhibition. No matter how good your work is, people need to know about it in order to attend and engage with it.

Creating a Social Media Marketing Campaign

Social media platforms like Instagram, Facebook, and even LinkedIn can be invaluable tools for promoting your exhibition. Start your campaign early—ideally 4-6 weeks before the show—so that people have plenty of time to plan.

Content Calendar: Create a posting schedule to build momentum leading up to the event. Start with teaser posts showcasing works in progress, behind-the-scenes studio shots, and glimpses of the exhibition venue. As the exhibition approaches, increase the frequency of posts and share finished works, personal stories about the creation process, and any press coverage the show is receiving.

Use features like Instagram Stories or Reels to create excitement and engagement. Consider hosting a live Q&A session a few days before the show to discuss your process, answer questions, and build a sense of anticipation.

Engage with Followers: Respond to comments, ask your followers for their thoughts, and encourage them to share your posts with others. You can even create polls or questions to build interaction and get your audience involved in the process.

Press Outreach and Media Coverage

In addition to social media, consider reaching out to local and national art publications, blogs, and newspapers. A press release is a great way to alert the media to your upcoming exhibition.

Write a compelling press release that includes all the essential details (dates, venue, key themes of the exhibition) and a personal artist statement. Include high-resolution images of your work and links to your website or social media.

Follow up with journalists or editors to gauge their interest, and if possible, offer an exclusive interview or feature. Coverage in even a small art blog or local newspaper can help increase foot traffic and online engagement for your exhibition.

Engaging with Visitors and Networking

Once the exhibition is open, it's time to engage with visitors and network with potential buyers, collectors, and gallery owners. Your presence at the event is crucial, not just for making sales but for building long-term relationships.

Conversations with Visitors: Not everyone who attends your exhibition will be familiar with your work, so be prepared to talk about it in an approachable and engaging way. You don't need to prepare a script, but having a few key talking points can help. Focus on what inspired the pieces, the techniques you used, and the overall themes of the exhibition.

Ask visitors open-ended questions, such as "What draws you to this piece?" or "Which work resonates with you the most?" This can spark deeper conversations and help potential buyers feel more connected to your art.

Avoid using overly technical language or art jargon that might alienate visitors. Keep your explanations clear and accessible, and let your passion for your work come through naturally.

Networking with Collectors and Galleries: Exhibitions are excellent opportunities for networking. Collectors often attend gallery shows to discover new artists, and many are interested in developing long-term relationships with artists whose work they admire.

If a visitor expresses interest in a particular piece, take the time to talk with them about it. Collect their contact information for follow-ups, even if they don't make a purchase immediately. Stay professional but friendly—making a strong personal connection can lead to future sales.

For gallery owners and curators, use the exhibition as a chance to showcase your professionalism and dedication. Engage in conversations about your career and artistic journey, and express interest in potential future collaborations. Follow up after the exhibition with a thank-you note or email to maintain these connections.

Managing Sales After the Exhibition

Making a sale at an exhibition is a wonderful feeling, but it's only the beginning of the sales process. After the exhibition ends, you'll need to handle the logistics of delivering sold artworks, following up with buyers, and maintaining your relationship with collectors.

Packaging and Shipping: Properly packaging your artwork is crucial to ensure it arrives safely at its destination. Use high-quality packing materials, especially for fragile works like glass-framed pieces or sculptures. Many professional art shippers offer custom packaging services, which can be a great option for valuable or delicate works.

For international sales, make sure you're familiar with customs regulations and taxes. Some countries have restrictions on the import or export of artwork, so it's important to check the requirements in advance. You'll also need to provide accurate documentation, such as invoices and certificates of authenticity.

Follow-Up with Buyers: After the sale, follow up with buyers to ensure they're satisfied with their purchase. Sending a handwritten thank-you note or email can help solidify the relationship and encourage future purchases. Keep buyers on your mailing list for updates about new works, exhibitions, or special offers.

Building Long-Term Relationships with Galleries

If your exhibition was held at a gallery, maintaining a good relationship with the gallery owner is key to securing future opportunities. Stay in touch with regular updates about your work and career. Attend other exhibitions at the gallery and engage with their artists and community. Building a long-term relationship can lead to more solo exhibitions, representation, and increased exposure.

Action Points

- Start planning your exhibition 4-6 months in advance, selecting a cohesive body of work that tells a story or fits the theme.

- Choose high-quality frames and ensure your artwork is presented in the best possible way with proper lighting and placement.
- Set competitive and consistent prices based on market research, your experience, and the complexity of your work.
- Create a social media marketing campaign to promote your exhibition, using behind-the-scenes content and engagement strategies.
- Reach out to local and national art publications for potential press coverage.
- Be approachable and engaging with visitors, focusing on your artistic inspiration and process in conversations.
- Network with collectors and galleries, collecting contact information for future follow-ups.
- Ensure proper packaging and shipping for sold artworks and stay informed about international sales regulations.
- Maintain long-term relationships with galleries through regular communication and participation in their events.

9

Branding for Artists

Branding is one of the most powerful tools an artist can have. It's not just about creating a catchy logo or a visually appealing website—branding is about shaping how the world perceives you and your work. In today's competitive art world, a strong and consistent brand helps you stand out, communicate your unique identity, and build lasting connections with collectors, galleries, and your audience.

By developing a strong, consistent brand, you'll build recognition, trust, and connection with your audience—helping you stand out in the art world and create a lasting, meaningful presence.

What Is an Artist Brand?

Your brand is the essence of who you are as an artist. It includes not only the visual aspects of your work, like color palettes and subject matter, but also the deeper story behind your art. It's the emotions you evoke, the message you communicate, and the way your audience connects with you on a personal level. Successful branding ties together everything you create and communicate, both in your art and in how you present yourself to the world.

Think of your brand as a promise to your audience. It tells them what to expect from your work, what you stand for, and why your art matters. A strong brand helps potential buyers understand who you are, what you value, and why they should invest in your work.

Why Branding Matters for Artists

In a crowded art market, it's not enough to create beautiful work. Your brand helps you cut through the noise and capture attention. When people feel a connection with you and your brand, they are more likely to remember you, follow your career, and ultimately buy your work. A consistent, recognizable brand builds trust, loyalty, and recognition, all of which are essential for long-term success.

Consider how branding can:

- **Create Recognition**: When people see your work or hear your name, your brand should come to mind immediately. This is how iconic artists become known—they are consistent in how they present themselves and their work.
- **Build Trust**: A strong, consistent brand helps establish

credibility and professionalism. When collectors and galleries see that you have a clear identity, they are more likely to trust in the quality and value of your work.

- **Attract the Right Audience**: Not every art lover will resonate with your work, and that's okay. Your brand helps you attract the people who truly connect with your style and message, creating a more loyal and engaged audience.

Defining Your Brand as an Artist

Building a brand starts with understanding who you are as an artist. To create a compelling and authentic brand, you need to dig deep into your motivations, values, and goals. Here are key questions to ask yourself as you define your brand:

- **What is my artistic vision?** What themes, stories, or emotions do I explore in my work? How do I want people to feel when they engage with my art?
- **What sets my work apart?** What makes my style, techniques, or subjects unique? What is the signature look or feel of my art?
- **Who is my audience?** Who do I want to connect with through my art? Are they collectors, casual buyers, or art enthusiasts? Knowing your audience helps you tailor your brand to resonate with them.
- **What values guide my work?** Do I focus on environmental issues, social justice, personal narratives,

or abstract concepts? Your values should be a core part of your brand.

By answering these questions, you can start to form a clear picture of your brand. Your goal is to create a cohesive identity that reflects both your artistic work and your personal story.

Examples of Strong Artist Brands

To give you a sense of how artists build strong brands, let's look at a couple of examples:

- **Frida Kahlo**: Her brand is built on her deeply personal, autobiographical work, which reflects pain, identity, and Mexican culture. Her distinctive style and symbolism, along with her iconic self-portraits, create a clear and recognizable brand.
- **Yayoi Kusama**: Known for her obsessive use of dots and immersive installations, Kusama's brand is rooted in repetition and infinity. Her signature polka dots and mirrored rooms have become symbols of her artistic identity, making her instantly recognizable in the art world.

These artists have built strong, memorable brands that reflect not only their artistic style but also their personal stories and values.

Crafting Your Visual Identity

Once you've defined the core elements of your brand, it's time to translate that into a visual identity. Your visual brand is what people see when they interact with your work—both online and in person. It includes your logo, website, color palette, typography, and the overall aesthetic of your materials. Below are the key elements of visual branding.

- **Logo**: Your logo should be simple, memorable, and reflective of your art. It could be as straightforward as a stylized version of your name or something more abstract that represents your artistic themes.

- **Color Palette**: Choose a color palette that reflects your art. If your work is bold and vibrant, consider using bright, energetic colors in your branding. If your work is more subdued, you might opt for neutral or pastel tones. Consistency in your color scheme across your website, social media, and printed materials reinforces your brand.

- **Typography**: The fonts you use should complement your art. A minimalist, sans-serif font might suit a modern artist, while a more decorative font could work for someone whose work is playful or whimsical. Keep it simple and ensure that your fonts are easy to read.

- **Photography and Imagery**: High-quality images of your work are essential to your brand. Make sure the photography you use captures the essence of your art. Consider how the images are styled and how they fit within your overall aesthetic.

- **Consistency**: The key to strong branding is consistency. Your website, social media profiles, business cards, and any other materials should all look and feel cohesive. When people see your brand, they should immediately recognize it as yours.

Example: Translating Your Brand into a Website

If you're an artist who focuses on environmental themes, your website could reflect this by using earthy tones like greens, browns, and blues. Your logo might incorporate a natural element, like a leaf or wave, and your photography could feature your art in natural settings, perhaps outdoors or in your studio with natural light. The typography would be clean and modern, reinforcing the message of sustainability.

Communicating Your Brand's Story

A strong visual brand is important, but branding goes deeper than aesthetics. Your brand story—the narrative that explains who you are and what you stand for—is what will truly connect with your audience on a personal level. This is where your personal story, motivations, and values come into play.

Your brand story should answer questions like:

- **Why do I create the art I create?**
- **What experiences or ideas have shaped my artistic journey?**
- **What do I hope people take away from my work?**

When you share this story, you humanize your brand and make it more relatable. Whether you're telling your story on your website, in an artist statement, or through social media posts, it should always feel authentic and aligned with your values.

For instance, if you started painting as a way to cope with a difficult time in your life, share that. If your work is inspired by your travels, talk about how those experiences shape your art. The more personal and genuine your story, the stronger the emotional connection with your audience will be.

Branding Across Platforms

Your brand needs to be consistent across every platform where people encounter your work, whether it's in person or online. This includes:

- **Website**: Your website is your digital gallery and the cornerstone of your brand. Make sure it's professionally designed, easy to navigate, and aligned with your visual identity.
- **Social Media**: Platforms like Instagram, Facebook, and TikTok are great tools for reinforcing your brand. Be consistent in how you present your work, interact with your followers, and use imagery and language that fits your brand's voice.
- **Print Materials**: Business cards, postcards, exhibition catalogs, and other print materials should also reflect

your brand. Ensure the design is cohesive with your digital presence, using the same fonts, colors, and tone.

- **Exhibitions and Shows**: Even your physical presence at shows and exhibitions should reinforce your brand. Consider how your booth is styled, how you interact with visitors, and how your promotional materials are displayed.

Action Points

- **Define Your Brand**: Reflect on your artistic vision, values, and goals to create a clear, authentic brand that resonates with your audience.
- **Develop a Visual Identity**: Create a cohesive visual brand that includes a logo, color palette, typography, and high-quality images of your work.
- **Craft Your Brand Story**: Share the personal narrative behind your art to create an emotional connection with your audience.
- **Consistency Across Platforms**: Ensure your website, social media profiles, print materials, and exhibitions all reflect your brand consistently.
- **Evolve Your Brand**: As your art evolves, your brand may evolve too. Stay true to your core identity, but allow for growth and change as your work and career develop.

10

Navigating Online Art Markets

In today's digital-first world, online art markets have revolutionized the way artists present, sell, and promote their work. These platforms have become vital tools for building exposure, reaching a global audience, and establishing direct connections with collectors and art lovers, bypassing traditional gallery systems. However, effectively navigating online art markets requires careful planning, strategy, and adaptability.

By mastering the intricacies of online art markets, you can build a global audience, increase your sales, and create a thriving art business. Embrace these tools to share your work with the world and unlock new opportunities for success.

The Power of Online Art Markets

Online art platforms have democratized access to the global art market, allowing artists to engage directly with buyers, collectors, and curators from around the world. Artists no longer need to rely solely on galleries to sell their work. Instead, they can create their own opportunities to showcase art on their terms.

The reach of online art markets extends far beyond local galleries. Through platforms like Etsy, Saatchi Art, and Redbubble, artists can sell works to buyers in different time zones, countries, and continents. This provides the opportunity for recurring income streams, whether through selling prints, originals, or licensing designs. Additionally, online markets give you control over how your work is presented, how often you update your inventory, and how you communicate with collectors.

For emerging and established artists alike, this presents an unprecedented opportunity to scale their business, grow their brand, and diversify income streams.

Choosing the Right Online Platform for Your Art

The first step in navigating online art markets is choosing the right platform. Each platform serves different purposes, audiences, and price points. Some focus on affordable prints and merchandise, while others cater to high-end collectors of original works. Understanding the strengths and weaknesses of each platform will help you make an informed choice.

1. Etsy

Etsy is one of the largest online marketplaces for handmade, vintage, and unique goods, including original art, prints, and customized products.

- **Target Audience**: Shoppers looking for affordable, unique, handmade goods, home decor, and art.
- **Best For**: Artists selling smaller works, prints, or customized art products like greeting cards, textiles, or jewelry. It's ideal for artists with a lower price point or those who offer multiple types of items beyond fine art.
- **Pros**: Easy to use, wide global audience, relatively low listing fees, customizable storefront, and strong search features. Etsy's search algorithms also favor sellers who regularly update their listings.
- **Cons**: Intense competition, lower price expectations from buyers, and it can be difficult to stand out unless you heavily market your shop.

2. Saatchi Art

As a major global platform, Saatchi Art focuses on high-quality, original works and limited-edition prints.

- **Target Audience**: Mid- to high-end collectors, galleries, and interior designers looking for investment-worthy pieces.
- **Best For**: Professional artists offering original paintings, sculptures, and fine art photography.

- **Pros**: Global visibility with a focus on curating high-quality art, offering artists the chance to work with interior designers and curators.
- **Cons**: Higher commission rates (up to 35%) and intense competition from established artists.

3. Artfinder

Artfinder is a global platform specifically for selling original art, connecting artists with collectors.

- **Target Audience**: Collectors seeking unique, one-of-a-kind original works.
- **Best For**: Artists with a focus on high-quality, original works across various mediums—painting, photography, sculpture, etc.
- **Pros**: Curation and marketing support, the ability to interact with buyers, and a focus on supporting independent artists.
- **Cons**: Higher fees than Etsy, competition from both emerging and well-established artists.

4. Redbubble and Society6

These print-on-demand platforms allow artists to sell their designs on various products, from wall art to home décor and apparel.

- **Target Audience**: Shoppers looking for unique,

affordable products featuring original designs. Appeals to younger audiences interested in pop culture, home decor, and personal accessories.

- **Best For**: Artists looking to sell prints and designs on products like t-shirts, phone cases, and wall art, or for those interested in passive income streams.
- **Pros**: No upfront production costs, ability to reach a large audience without needing to manage inventory, and an easy entry into print-on-demand.
- **Cons**: Lower profit margins due to production and platform fees, limited opportunity to sell high-priced original works, and more suited to commercial artists.

5. Fine Art America

Fine Art America operates as both a print-on-demand platform and a gallery for artists selling original work.

- **Target Audience**: Art buyers looking for prints and framed art, with some demand for original work.
- **Best For**: Artists seeking a mix of print sales and originals, as well as those looking to sell commercial items such as framed prints, home decor, and art-themed gifts.
- **Pros**: Wide variety of product options, integration with marketplaces like Amazon, and a built-in audience for prints.
- **Cons**: High competition, with more of a focus on lower-cost items like prints than original, high-end art.

6. *LinkedIn*

Though traditionally seen as a professional networking site, LinkedIn has growing relevance for artists looking to connect with galleries, curators, corporate buyers, and art consultants.

- **Target Audience**: Corporate buyers, galleries, curators, and other industry professionals.
- **Best For**: Building professional connections and seeking gallery representation or corporate commissions.
- **Pros**: LinkedIn's network offers opportunities to establish credibility, promote your career, and make business connections that can lead to exhibitions and collaborations.
- **Cons**: LinkedIn's audience is more business-focused, which means it may not drive direct sales of artwork in the way other platforms do.

Creating an Optimized Online Presence

Once you've selected your platform(s), creating a professional and optimized profile is key to standing out and converting visitors into buyers. Your online presence should reflect your artistic brand and make it easy for potential buyers to find, connect with, and purchase your work.

1. *High-Quality Images and Visuals*

The most important element of your online portfolio is the visual representation of your work. Poor-quality images can detract from the appeal of your artwork, making even the best pieces look unprofessional. To maximize visual impact:

- Use high-resolution images (at least 1500 pixels wide) to ensure clarity on all screen sizes.
- Show multiple angles of your work, especially for sculptures or pieces with intricate textures.
- Include close-up shots to highlight details like brush-strokes, texture, or intricate patterns.
- Use neutral backgrounds to keep the focus on the art itself.

2. Crafting Compelling Descriptions

Each piece should have a detailed and engaging description. Don't just list the size and materials—tell the story behind the work. What inspired you? What emotions or ideas are you conveying? Buyers are drawn to the narrative behind art, which can influence their decision to purchase.

Here are a few tips for creating effective descriptions:

- **Tell a story**: Share the inspiration, concept, or personal significance of the work.
- **Be specific**: Include dimensions, materials, and any relevant process details, such as techniques you used or time spent on the piece.
- **Highlight uniqueness**: Why is this piece special? Explain what makes it one of a kind.

3. Pricing Strategy

Pricing your work correctly is crucial, particularly in the online art market where comparisons are easy. Research similar pieces on the platform and evaluate your competition. Be sure to factor in platform fees, shipping, taxes, and materials. Offering flexible payment options (installment plans or layaway) can help you appeal to more buyers for higher-priced pieces.

4. SEO for Artists

Online platforms often function like search engines, so understanding SEO (Search Engine Optimization) is key to making your work discoverable. Use relevant keywords in your artwork titles and descriptions, such as "contemporary abstract painting" or "landscape oil painting." Avoid vague titles like "Untitled" without a subtitle that provides more context.

5. Building Your Artist Profile

Your artist profile is your opportunity to make a personal connection with buyers. Include a well-written artist bio, a professional headshot, and a clear statement of your artistic vision. Buyers want to know who the artist is behind the work, so take the time to share your journey, inspiration, and any notable exhibitions or accolades.

Marketing Your Art Online

Simply listing your work on an online platform is not enough to generate sales. You need to actively promote your online presence through a multi-faceted marketing strategy.

1. Social Media Promotion

Platforms like Instagram, Pinterest, and TikTok are powerful tools for driving traffic to your online store. Regularly share high-quality images and videos of your work, behind-the-scenes content, and stories about your creative process to engage your audience.

2. Email Marketing

Build an email list of collectors, fans, and followers and send them regular updates. Use newsletters to share new works, exclusive sales, or invitations to virtual exhibitions. Email marketing allows you to engage directly with your audience without relying on social media algorithms.

3. Collaborations

Partnering with other artists or influencers in your niche can help you reach new audiences. Collaborative projects, giveaways, or cross-promotions introduce your work to followers of other artists, which can drive traffic and increase your visibility.

4. Paid Advertising

Consider using paid ads on social media platforms or within the art marketplace itself. Facebook and Instagram ads allow you to target specific demographics, interests, and geographic regions. Many online art platforms also offer internal promotion options where you can pay for greater visibility.

Offering Excellent Customer Service

Good customer service sets you apart in online art markets, ensuring positive experiences that encourage repeat buyers and referrals. This involves transparent communication, efficient processes, and an overall smooth transaction from start to finish.

1. Clear Shipping and Return Policies

Make your shipping, handling, and return policies clear upfront. Buyers want to know how long it will take for their piece to arrive, how it will be packaged, and what to do if there's a problem. Offer tracking numbers, provide insurance for valuable works, and be transparent about shipping costs. Having a clear return policy also builds buyer trust.

2. Handling Customer Inquiries

Respond promptly to customer inquiries about your work. Whether it's a question about dimensions, materials, or availability, timely and professional communication can make the difference between a sale and a lost opportunity. Acknowledge all messages within 24 hours and keep buyers updated throughout the purchasing process.

3. Resolving Disputes

Unfortunately, issues like shipping damage or buyer dissatisfaction can arise. Address these issues with professionalism and promptness. Offer solutions such as repairs, replacements, or refunds when appropriate, and work with buyers to find a resolution that leaves them satisfied.

Tracking Your Progress

Tracking your performance is key to refining your approach and growing your online art business.

1. Tracking Sales and Metrics

Most online platforms offer analytics to track how many views your listings are getting, where your traffic is coming from, and how many of those visitors are converting into sales. Pay close attention to the performance of individual pieces to identify trends in what resonates with buyers.

2. Adapting Based on Data

Adjust your strategies based on the data you collect. If certain styles or price points perform better, consider focusing more on those areas. Test different approaches—alter descriptions, change your pricing strategy, or update your photos—and measure the impact of those changes.

Action Points

- Research and select the best online platforms for your art based on your target audience and artistic goals.
- Create high-quality images and detailed descriptions for each piece to attract buyers.
- Optimize your listings for search engines using relevant keywords and clear titles.
- Use social media and email marketing to drive traffic to your online store.
- Provide excellent customer service with clear shipping, return policies, and prompt communication.
- Track your performance, adjust your strategies, and refine your approach based on metrics and buyer feedback.

11

Customer Relationship Management

Building strong relationships with your customers is key to sustaining your art career. Whether you sell through galleries, online platforms, art fairs, or directly from your studio, the quality of your interactions with buyers can be the difference between a one-time sale and a long-term supporter. Customer Relations Management (CRM) involves understanding your customers' needs, creating a seamless and personal buying experience, and building connections that lead to repeat sales, word-of-mouth referrals, and loyal patrons.

CRM, for an artist, is about more than selling—it's about creating a community around your art, nurturing relationships, and establishing trust that lasts long after the transaction. With the right approach to Customer Relations

Management, you'll not only grow your network of buyers but also build lasting relationships that support the growth of your art business for years to come. By focusing on personalized interactions, maintaining professionalism, and fostering emotional connections with your audience, you create an art business that's built on trust, loyalty, and meaningful relationships.

Why CRM Is Critical for Artists

In a competitive art world, having a solid body of work is only part of the equation. Many artists wonder why their art isn't selling as well as they'd hoped, despite putting hours into their craft. The answer often lies in the relationships they build—or fail to build—with their audience. In many cases, people buy art because they connect with the artist as much as with the artwork itself. This is where CRM comes into play.

Good CRM fosters loyalty, which results in more than just one-time purchases. When people have a positive experience buying from you, they're more likely to talk about your work, recommend you to friends, and become repeat customers. These connections also lead to invaluable opportunities like commissions, collaborations, and invitations to exhibit at prestigious venues.

For artists, customer relationships aren't just about the transaction; they're about developing a following of dedicated patrons who are invested in your success.

Creating a Personal Connection

Building personal connections with your buyers is vital. Art is an emotional purchase, often driven by a personal connection with the artist or the story behind a piece. When buyers feel like they know you or understand your work on a deeper level, they're more likely to make a purchase and support your career over time.

1. Storytelling: The Heart of Customer Engagement

Storytelling is one of the most powerful ways to connect with your audience. When you share the stories behind your art—whether it's what inspired you, your artistic process, or the challenges you faced during creation—you create a narrative that engages people emotionally. This goes beyond simply appreciating your technique; it allows buyers to feel like they are part of your journey.

Artists can incorporate storytelling into:

- **Art Descriptions**: Use your website or social media to write engaging descriptions for each piece, explaining its inspiration or the thought process behind it.
- **Social Media**: Post regular updates about your artistic journey, your creative process, or the things that inspire your work.
- **In-Person Interactions**: At art shows or fairs, tell visitors the backstory of specific pieces when they

show interest. This can turn casual conversations into meaningful connections.

Storytelling not only creates a personal bond but also adds intrinsic value to the artwork. Collectors often appreciate knowing the meaning behind a piece, which makes it more than just a visual object—it becomes a part of their personal narrative.

2. Personalized Communication

As you grow your list of collectors and interested buyers, personalizing your communication with them will help maintain and strengthen the relationship. Tailor your interactions based on their preferences. For instance, if you know that a buyer loves abstract art, keep them informed about new works in that genre. If someone bought a piece related to a specific theme (such as landscapes), update them when similar works become available.

Use personalized touches such as:

- **Handwritten Thank-You Notes**: After a sale, send a personal note thanking the buyer. This gesture makes buyers feel appreciated and adds a human touch to the transaction.
- **Customized Emails**: When sending out newsletters or promotional materials, segment your mailing list so collectors receive relevant content based on their interests.

- **Exclusive Previews**: Offer your most loyal customers early access to new collections, special pricing, or the opportunity to commission custom pieces. This fosters a sense of exclusivity and rewards their loyalty.

3. Regular Updates

Your CRM strategy should include regular communication with your audience. This could take the form of email newsletters, social media posts, or even personal outreach for high-value collectors. Regular updates help keep your audience engaged with your work and aware of new projects, exhibitions, or pieces for sale.

Tips for maintaining regular updates:

- **Email Newsletters**: Use email marketing tools like Mailchimp to send regular newsletters featuring new works, behind-the-scenes insights, or upcoming exhibitions. This keeps you top-of-mind with your audience.
- **Social Media**: Be active on platforms like Instagram, Facebook, or LinkedIn. Regular posting helps maintain engagement and shows collectors that you're continuously producing new work.
- **Personal Check-Ins**: For top collectors or repeat buyers, consider reaching out personally to check in, share updates, or let them know about new pieces before they're released to the public.

Managing Inquiries and Sales Communication

Handling inquiries professionally and promptly is crucial for turning potential buyers into customers. How you respond to inquiries reflects your professionalism and can make or break a sale.

1. Responding to Inquiries

Whether someone contacts you via email, social media, or through your website, respond as quickly as possible. Delays in responding can lead to lost opportunities, especially if the potential buyer is browsing multiple artists.

When responding:

- **Be Prompt and Professional**: Always respond within 24 hours when possible. Your message should be courteous, clear, and informative.
- **Provide Complete Information**: When someone asks about a piece, provide details about the size, medium, price, and any relevant backstory. If applicable, include information about shipping costs and timelines.
- **Offer Next Steps**: If someone expresses interest but isn't ready to purchase, offer a clear call to action, such as scheduling a studio visit, providing additional images, or discussing payment options.

For example: "Thank you for your interest in my work!

The piece you inquired about, *Sunset Glow*, is a 24x36-inch acrylic painting on canvas, priced at $1,500. Shipping is free within the U.S., and I can send you additional close-up images if you'd like. Let me know if you'd like to move forward or if you have any other questions!"

2. Handling Commissions

Commissioned work is a great way to build relationships with collectors, but it requires clear communication to ensure expectations are aligned. Managing commissions well can lead to repeat business and recommendations.

When managing commissions:

- **Discuss Expectations Clearly**: Before starting, outline the scope of the work, including the size, style, subject matter, timeline, and price.
- **Provide Regular Updates**: Keep the client updated on your progress, sharing images of the work at different stages. This not only keeps them engaged but also ensures you're meeting their expectations.
- **Handle Revisions Professionally**: If the client requests changes during the process, be open to feedback but make sure to manage expectations. Discuss what's possible within the agreed-upon scope and any potential changes to the timeline or cost.

Delivering a Seamless Buying Experience

A smooth, professional buying experience is essential for building trust and encouraging future purchases. Whether you sell online, through galleries, or directly to buyers, each step of the process should reflect care and professionalism.

1. Streamlined Payment and Shipping

Ensure your payment options are straightforward and easy to use. Offering various payment methods—credit cards, PayPal, wire transfers—gives buyers flexibility. For higher-priced works, offering installment plans can open the door to more buyers who might not be able to pay upfront.

For shipping:

- **Secure Packaging**: Invest in high-quality packaging to protect the artwork during transit. Use bubble wrap, corner protectors, and sturdy boxes to ensure the piece arrives undamaged.
- **Provide Tracking Information**: Once the artwork has been shipped, send the buyer tracking information so they can monitor the delivery. This level of communication helps reassure the buyer and adds a level of professionalism.
- **Include a Personal Touch**: Add a thank-you note, care instructions, and perhaps a small token, like a postcard or print of your work. These touches enhance

the unboxing experience and reinforce the connection between artist and buyer.

2. Post-Sale Follow-Up

Following up after a sale is crucial. Not only does it show that you appreciate the buyer's support, but it also opens the door to future sales and recommendations. A simple thank-you email after delivery can make a significant impact.

Your follow-up should:

- **Thank the Buyer**: Express gratitude for their support.
- **Ask for Feedback**: Encourage them to share their thoughts on the piece and their buying experience. Positive feedback can be used as testimonials on your website or social media.
- **Offer Future Engagement**: Let them know how to stay connected, whether through social media, email updates, or studio visits.

Handling Customer Complaints with Care

No matter how careful you are, issues can arise. Whether it's a damaged shipment or a buyer who feels unsatisfied, how you handle complaints will determine whether you can maintain the relationship.

1. *Acknowledge the Complaint Quickly*

Respond to any complaints as soon as possible. A timely acknowledgment shows the customer that you take their concerns seriously and are committed to resolving the issue.

2. *Offer Solutions*

Depending on the situation, offer practical solutions:

- **For Shipping Issues**: If the artwork arrives damaged, offer a refund, a replacement, or a repair (if feasible). Make sure to apologize for the inconvenience and handle any additional shipping costs.
- **For Artistic Disagreements**: If a buyer is unsatisfied with a commissioned piece, address their concerns and offer revisions within reason. Discuss upfront how many revisions you're willing to make and set boundaries to avoid endless adjustments.

Tools for Managing Customer Relations

While personal connection is important, technology can help you stay organized and manage multiple customer relationships efficiently.

1. Customer Relationship Management Software

CRM tools are designed to help businesses manage their interactions with clients. While traditionally used by larger businesses, CRM software can be useful for artists who want to track their collectors, manage inquiries, and stay organized. Popular CRM options include:

- **HubSpot CRM**: Offers free tools for contact management, email tracking, and scheduling follow-up tasks.
- **Salesforce**: A powerful CRM tool that allows for detailed tracking of customer interactions, but it may be more complex than what most artists need.
- **Airtable**: A flexible tool that can be customized to create a simple database for tracking customer relationships and artwork sales.

2. Social Media Management Tools

If you're active on multiple social media platforms, tools like Buffer or Hootsuite can help you stay on top of interactions. These tools allow you to schedule posts, respond to messages, and track engagement from a single dashboard.

Action Points

- Maintain an up-to-date customer database, including preferences, past purchases, and contact information, to create personalized interactions.

- Develop a post-sale follow-up strategy that includes thank-you notes, feedback requests, and future engagement opportunities.
- Create an emotional connection with your audience by sharing the stories behind your work and inviting them into your creative process.
- Respond promptly and professionally to inquiries, complaints, and feedback, ensuring a positive customer experience.
- Explore CRM tools like HubSpot or Airtable to stay organized, track interactions, and maintain strong relationships with your buyers.
- Offer personalized touches such as handwritten notes, exclusive previews, and loyalty perks to strengthen your relationships with key collectors.
- Regularly update your audience through newsletters and social media, ensuring that they remain engaged with your work over time.

12

Building Relationships: Networking, Collaborations, and Partnerships

In the art world, relationships are often the foundation for success. Whether it's forming connections with other artists, galleries, collectors, or corporate partners, networking and collaboration are essential tools for building visibility, creating opportunities, and fostering long-term growth. By cultivating authentic relationships, you not only increase your chances of finding new opportunities, but you also create a community of support around your art practice.

By investing in building relationships, collaborating with others, and forming strategic partnerships, you will create a thriving network that can support your artistic journey for years to come. Whether through personal networking or professional partnerships, these connections will help you grow, create new opportunities, and achieve long-term success in the art world.

The Importance of Building Relationships

Relationships matter more than ever in the art world. A personal recommendation or a well-timed introduction can lead to significant opportunities, from securing gallery representation to landing a commission or exhibition. Relationships also play a role in growing your credibility. When collectors or galleries see that other artists, curators, or influencers support your work, it strengthens your reputation and builds trust.

While networking might feel daunting or transactional at first, the key is to approach it as a way to build genuine, long-lasting relationships. Think of networking as relationship-building rather than just an exchange of business cards. Your goal is to connect with people who can help advance your career, but who you can also support in return, creating a mutually beneficial relationship over time.

Networking: Making Authentic Connections

Networking, whether online or in person, is one of the most effective ways to advance your art career. Through networking, you can connect with collectors, galleries, other artists, curators, art consultants, and even potential mentors. Effective networking isn't about forcing yourself into conversations; it's about building meaningful relationships based on mutual interests and shared goals.

1. Assess Your Current Network

Before you dive into expanding your network, take stock of the connections you already have. Consider your existing relationships and whether there are people you could reconnect with or deepen your relationship with. Ask yourself:

- Who in my current network can introduce me to new opportunities?
- Are there any relationships I've neglected that I should revisit?
- What are the gaps in my network? Do I need more connections with collectors, gallery owners, or other artists?

By starting with the relationships you already have, you can build a strong foundation before reaching out to new people.

2. How to Network Effectively at Art Events

Attending gallery openings, art fairs, and exhibitions is one of the best ways to connect with others in the art world. Here are some practical tips for maximizing your networking at these events:

- **Research the event**: Before attending, find out who will be there. Look at the artists featured, the galleries represented, and any industry professionals who may attend. Having background knowledge will give you talking points and help you focus on making the most important connections.

- **Be approachable and friendly**: Smile, make eye contact, and don't be afraid to strike up conversations with strangers. People attend these events expecting to meet others, so it's natural to introduce yourself. Keep your introduction short and engaging: "Hi, I'm [Name], an abstract artist working primarily in acrylic. I love how this exhibition explores different mediums—what do you think of it?"

- **Follow up**: After the event, follow up with the people you met by sending a brief email or message. Mention something specific from your conversation to personalize the message, and suggest staying in touch for potential collaborations or opportunities.

3. Using Social Media for Networking

Online networking is a powerful tool that allows you to reach a broader audience and connect with art world professionals globally. Platforms like Instagram, LinkedIn, and Twitter can serve as effective networking hubs if used strategically.

- **Instagram**: Engage with artists, galleries, and collectors by liking and commenting on their posts. When you leave a comment, take the time to make your engagement meaningful. For example, instead of a generic "Great work," you could say something more specific like, "I love how you captured the texture in this piece—it adds so much depth." Over time, these interactions can lead to deeper connections as well as potential collaborations.

- **LinkedIn**: Use LinkedIn to connect with art consultants, gallery owners, and curators. Be sure your LinkedIn profile reflects your professional journey as an artist and clearly communicates your artistic identity. Engage in discussions in relevant LinkedIn groups or forums, such as those for contemporary art or artist networks.

- **Twitter**: Twitter can be used to network with art critics, writers, and curators. By sharing insights, engaging with trending art-related conversations, and participating in live Twitter chats about art, you can create valuable connections.

- **Clubhouse or Art-Focused Forums**: Platforms like Clubhouse offer real-time discussions on topics related to the art world. Joining rooms related to art marketing, art exhibitions, or creative processes allows you to connect with industry professionals and other artists directly.

Collaborations: Enhancing Your Artistic Practice Through Joint Projects

Collaborating with other artists, galleries, or brands is one of the most effective ways to broaden your reach, expose your work to new audiences, and fuel creative growth. Collaborations often combine the strengths of both parties, leading to more innovative projects and a wider audience base for both.

1. The Benefits of Artist Collaborations

Collaborating can be a game-changer for your career. Here are some key benefits:

- **New Audiences**: By collaborating with another artist or brand, you introduce your work to their audience, expanding your reach beyond your current followers.
- **Creative Synergy**: Collaborating with another artist can bring fresh perspectives and ideas to your work, sparking new creativity and innovation.
- **Shared Resources**: When you collaborate, you often share studio space, materials, or marketing efforts, which can lower costs and streamline the production process.
- **Media Attention**: Joint projects, especially when they combine different art forms or genres, tend to attract media attention, increasing the visibility of your work.

2. Finding the Right Collaboration Partner

Finding the right collaborator is crucial to a successful project. Here are some factors to consider:

- **Aligned Visions**: Choose a collaborator whose artistic vision aligns with yours. The more you share in terms of values, aesthetic goals, and purpose, the smoother the collaboration will be.
- **Complementary Strengths**: Look for someone whose strengths complement your own. For example, if you're a painter, collaborating with a sculptor or multimedia artist could lead to an exciting cross-medium project.
- **Shared Audience**: If possible, find someone whose audience would be interested in your work as well. This ensures the collaboration benefits both parties by exposing each of you to a relevant new audience.

3. Examples of Successful Artist Collaborations

- **Joint Exhibitions**: Artists with complementary styles may collaborate on a joint exhibition, sharing the workload, costs, and audience. For instance, a painter and a photographer might collaborate on an exhibition that explores the theme of memory, with each artist bringing their own interpretation to the subject.
- **Multidisciplinary Collaborations**: Some artists collaborate across different disciplines to create immersive installations. A painter might team up with a

sound artist to create an interactive installation that incorporates both visual and auditory elements, drawing visitors into a multi-sensory experience.

- **Collaborating with Brands**: Artists can collaborate with brands for commercial projects, such as designing limited-edition products, working on advertising campaigns, or creating branded art pieces. These partnerships can provide significant exposure and additional income.

Partnerships: Strategic Alliances for Long-Term Success

Strategic partnerships go beyond one-off collaborations and can provide long-term support and opportunities. These partnerships may be with galleries, corporations, art consultants, or nonprofits. A strong partnership can provide ongoing exposure, financial backing, or a platform for larger-scale projects.

1. Partnering with Galleries

Partnering with a gallery can provide significant exposure and legitimacy. However, finding the right gallery—one that aligns with your style and values—is key.

- **Research Galleries**: Look for galleries that represent artists with work similar to yours or those who focus on your medium or genre. Attend gallery openings to observe the kinds of artists they represent and meet the gallery owners or curators.

- **Building Relationships with Galleries**: Introduce yourself at gallery events, participate in open calls, or send a polite and professional portfolio submission. Building rapport with a gallery takes time, but once you've established a relationship, you may be invited to participate in group shows or even offered representation.

2. Corporate Partnerships

More and more corporations are seeking partnerships with artists to enhance their branding, create unique experiences, or develop limited-edition products. Corporate partnerships can include commissioned works for office spaces, branded merchandise, or collaborative events.

- **Approaching Corporations**: To form a corporate partnership, research companies that align with your values or style. Consider crafting a proposal that outlines the mutual benefits of a partnership. For example, you might pitch your art for an upcoming corporate event, offering to create customized pieces or live-paint at the event.
- **Benefits of Corporate Partnerships**: Corporate partnerships provide financial stability, consistent exposure, and opportunities to expand into new markets.

Partnering with a well-known brand can also elevate your credibility within the art world.

3. Working with Art Consultants

Art consultants act as intermediaries between artists and buyers, often working with corporate clients, individual collectors, or interior designers to source art. Building relationships with consultants can lead to regular commissions and sales.

- **Finding Art Consultants**: Research art consultants who specialize in your genre or medium. Attend events, exhibitions, and art fairs where consultants are likely to be present. Once you've established a relationship, they can recommend your work to their clients or help you secure commissions.

Maintaining and Nurturing Your Relationships

Building relationships is only the first step. Maintaining and nurturing those connections is key to sustaining long-term success in your art career.

- **Consistent Communication**: Stay in touch with the people in your network through occasional emails, social media interactions, or in-person catch-ups. Show genuine interest in their work, and don't reach out only when you need something.

- **Supporting Others**: Support the people in your network by promoting their work, attending their exhibitions, or sharing opportunities with them. By giving as much as you receive, you'll build stronger, more reciprocal relationships.

Action Points

- Assess your current network and identify gaps in relationships that need nurturing or new connections that could help your art career.
- Attend local gallery openings, exhibitions, and art fairs to meet other artists, collectors, and gallery owners. Be proactive in starting conversations.
- Use social media platforms, such as Instagram, LinkedIn, and Twitter, to engage with artists, curators, and art professionals worldwide.
- Explore potential collaborations with other artists or brands to introduce your work to new audiences and spark creative growth.
- Research galleries and corporate partners that align with your style and values. Build relationships with them by attending events and submitting your portfolio when appropriate.
- Develop long-term partnerships with art consultants or corporations that can provide regular commissions or larger opportunities.

- Nurture relationships by staying in touch, offering support, and keeping communication open with the people in your network.

13

Exploring Multiple
Income Streams

A s an artist, relying solely on the sale of original pieces can limit your financial potential. In today's diversified economy, there are numerous opportunities to expand your income beyond traditional art sales. Exploring multiple income streams allows you to stabilize your earnings, reach new audiences, and ultimately gain more control over your career. By diversifying, you can continue growing your business while developing new skills, reducing financial risk, and tapping into untapped markets. You can reduce your reliance on any one form of revenue and build a more sustainable, flexible art practice.

Licensing Your Artwork

Licensing your artwork allows you to earn passive income by giving companies or individuals permission to use your art on their products, like apparel, home decor, stationery, or digital assets. It opens up a significant income stream, particularly when working with larger retail chains or popular online platforms.

To start with licensing, it's crucial to:

- **Understand Licensing Agreements:** When you license your artwork, you'll need to sign agreements that detail where and how your art can be used. Licensing contracts typically outline the scope of use, the duration of the agreement, royalties, and geographic limitations. You may be paid an upfront fee, ongoing royalties, or both.
- **Find the Right Partners:** There are companies specifically looking for unique art to place on their products. Some licensing agencies act as intermediaries, helping artists connect with such companies. Websites like Society6 and Redbubble allow you to upload your work and earn royalties on every sale without needing to manage production or distribution.
- **Maintain Ownership:** Licensing typically allows artists to retain the copyright of their work while granting the licensee permission to use it. This way, you can continue to sell your art in other capacities or license it to multiple companies in different industries.

Print-on-Demand (POD)

Print-on-demand is one of the easiest ways to generate additional income streams with minimal investment. POD platforms allow you to upload high-quality digital versions of your artwork, which are then printed on a range of products only when a customer orders them. This avoids the need for inventory or upfront costs and creates new avenues for people to purchase your art in forms like clothing, mugs, or canvas prints.

Key benefits of POD:

- **No Upfront Costs:** Since products are printed as they're ordered, you don't need to pay for inventory or handle shipping.
- **Global Reach:** Platforms like Society6, Printful, and Fine Art America allow your art to be available to buyers around the world.
- **Scalability:** Once you've uploaded your artwork, these platforms handle the rest, allowing you to scale with little ongoing effort.

To make the most of POD:

- **Offer a Range of Products:** Upload artwork in various dimensions and formats to appeal to different customer preferences. Some buyers may prefer large prints for their walls, while others might be interested in smaller, functional items like phone cases or notebooks.

- **Market Your Designs:** Promote your POD products on your website and social media channels. You'll need to drive traffic to your online store since these platforms don't always do the marketing for you.

Teaching and Workshops

Many artists earn a significant portion of their income by sharing their expertise through teaching, both online and in-person. Workshops, tutorials, and mentoring sessions provide ways to engage with your community while establishing yourself as an expert in your field.

There are a variety of ways to teach:

- **Host In-Person Workshops:** If you have a dedicated studio space or can rent a venue, consider organizing art workshops. These can range from beginner classes to more advanced technique sessions. You can charge for these workshops based on the materials provided, length of the session, and the depth of instruction.
- **Create Online Courses:** Online learning platforms like Skillshare, Teachable, or Udemy allow artists to create pre-recorded or live video courses on specific topics. You can teach others about painting techniques, digital art, or even the business side of art. Once uploaded, these courses can generate passive income over time.
- **Private Lessons:** For a more personalized teaching

experience, you might offer one-on-one mentorships or private art lessons, either in-person or online.

Selling Digital Products

Another way to diversify income streams is by creating and selling digital products related to your art. Digital products require little maintenance and no physical materials, and they can be sold repeatedly without incurring additional costs.

Types of digital products include:

- **Downloadable Art Prints:** Some buyers prefer instant gratification. By offering high-resolution downloadable art prints, you allow people to buy your work, print it themselves, and enjoy it immediately.
- **Digital Brushes and Art Assets:** If you're a digital artist, you can create and sell custom brushes or design assets that others can use in their own artwork. Platforms like Gumroad and Etsy are popular places to sell these items.
- **E-Books or Guides:** Consider creating instructional e-books, art tutorials, or even step-by-step guides on how you create your work. For instance, a guide on mastering watercolor techniques or understanding abstract composition could provide value to both fellow artists and collectors interested in your process.

Crowdfunding and Membership Platforms

Crowdfunding platforms like Kickstarter and Patreon can help you generate ongoing support from your fan base. These platforms work well if you have an engaged audience who is willing to support your work in exchange for exclusive rewards.

- **Kickstarter or Indiegogo:** These platforms are ideal if you're launching a specific project, like an exhibition, a new art series, or a book. Artists can create campaigns to raise funds, often by offering limited-edition rewards or early access to their work. Success on these platforms often depends on having an engaged audience and a compelling story.
- **Patreon:** Patreon allows artists to earn recurring monthly income from subscribers who are eager to support their ongoing work. In return for their support, patrons often receive exclusive content, behind-the-scenes updates, or early access to new pieces.

Non-Fungible Tokens (NFTs)

NFTs are a newer and potentially lucrative revenue stream for digital artists. NFTs are unique digital assets that represent ownership of a piece of art or collectible. Because of the blockchain technology behind them, NFTs allow digital artists to sell their work as one-of-a-kind or limited-edition items with proof of authenticity.

How to get started with NFTs:

- **Choose a Platform:** Platforms like OpenSea, Rarible, and Foundation allow you to mint and sell your NFTs. Each platform operates slightly differently, so it's important to research which one fits your needs.
- **Mint Your Artwork:** Minting is the process of turning your digital artwork into an NFT on the blockchain. This can come with initial costs (called "gas fees"), so plan accordingly.
- **Engage with the Community:** The NFT space thrives on community interaction. Actively engage with collectors, share your process, and promote your NFTs on social media platforms like Twitter and Discord.

Crowdfunding for Projects

Crowdfunding can offer a major boost for artists trying to fund larger projects. Platforms like Kickstarter and Go-FundMe allow you to rally your supporters and raise funds to complete specific pieces or projects. If you are looking to create a new body of work, mount a major exhibition, or self-publish a book, crowdfunding can help cover the costs in advance.

Crowdfunding strategies include:

- **Offer Unique Rewards:** People are more likely to contribute if they receive something in return. Offer limited-edition prints, original sketches, or behind-the-scenes access to your process as incentives for different funding levels.

- **Tell Your Story:** Success in crowdfunding often depends on the story behind your project. Be transparent about your goals and what their funding will help you achieve.
- **Engage Your Network:** Promote your campaign on your social media channels, website, and email list to engage potential backers.

Passive Income Through Stock Art

Stock art websites, like Shutterstock or Adobe Stock, allow you to upload and sell your artwork for others to use in their designs, publications, or websites. Artists typically earn royalties whenever their work is downloaded, providing a small but steady stream of income.

To succeed with stock art:

- **Upload Regularly:** Consistently uploading high-quality images increases the chances of your work being purchased.
- **Understand Trends:** Keep an eye on what's trending in the design world to ensure your stock art is relevant.
- **Diversify:** Include a variety of themes, colors, and styles to reach a broader audience.

Action Points

- Research licensing agencies and explore platforms like Society6 or Redbubble.
- Consider offering online courses or workshops to share your expertise.
- Develop digital products such as downloadable prints or custom design assets.
- Explore platforms like Patreon or Kickstarter to connect with supporters.
- Start learning about NFTs and consider minting your work for sale as digital collectibles.
- Upload work to stock art sites to generate passive income.

14

Print-on-Demand in the Art World

Print-on-demand (POD) has revolutionized how artists can sell their work. In the past, creating physical products required a significant upfront investment in printing and inventory, with the added challenge of managing shipping and fulfillment. However, POD platforms allow artists to sell customized products featuring their artwork without the need for inventory or overhead costs. This approach can significantly expand your revenue streams and reach a wider audience, all while maintaining flexibility and minimizing financial risks. By incorporating print-on-demand into your business model, you can reach new markets, increase your sales, and continue focusing on your art practice without the burden of managing physical inventory.

Understanding Print-on-Demand

Print-on-demand operates on a simple principle: you upload your artwork to a platform, and when a customer orders a product (such as a print, mug, T-shirt, or phone case), the platform prints the item, handles payment, and ships it directly to the customer. The benefit for artists is that you don't have to worry about holding inventory or managing logistics.

Key Benefits of POD:

- **No Inventory Risk:** You don't need to order large quantities of products upfront. Instead, each item is printed as it is sold.
- **Lower Costs:** Since you don't need to manage production or fulfillment, your costs are significantly lower than traditional retail models.
- **Global Reach:** POD platforms often have international fulfillment centers, allowing your work to reach buyers worldwide without additional shipping concerns.
- **Product Variety:** With POD, your artwork can be featured on a range of products beyond traditional prints, including clothing, home decor, stationery, and accessories.

Choosing the Right POD Platform

Not all POD platforms are created equal, and it's essential to choose the one that aligns best with your goals, audience, and the type of products you want to offer. Each platform has unique features, pricing structures, and product offerings, so consider what's most important for your business.

Here are some of the most popular POD platforms for artists:

1. Society6: Society6 is one of the most popular POD platforms for artists, offering a wide range of products, including art prints, home decor items, and lifestyle accessories. Artists can upload their artwork, set their own pricing for art prints, and earn a commission on every sale.

- **Pros:** Large product selection, built-in artist community, global reach.
- **Cons:** Lower commission rates for non-artwork items like home decor.

2. Redbubble: Redbubble is another well-known POD platform that allows artists to sell their work on a variety of products, including apparel, stickers, and phone cases. It's known for its ease of use and strong artist community.

- **Pros:** User-friendly interface, diverse product selection, easy to set up.
- **Cons:** Like Society6, artists earn lower commissions on certain product types.

3. Fine Art America: Fine Art America focuses more on traditional art prints and allows artists to offer high-quality framed prints, canvas art, and posters. The platform also has a POD offering for products like T-shirts, phone cases, and home decor.

- **Pros:** Higher quality art prints, options for framing and canvas prints, and customizable pricing for art prints.
- **Cons:** Limited product selection outside of traditional prints.

4. Printful: Printful integrates with your existing e-commerce store (such as Shopify or WooCommerce), offering more control over branding and marketing. You can create custom products, and Printful handles the fulfillment when orders are placed.

- **Pros:** Full branding control, integrates with multiple e-commerce platforms.
- **Cons:** Requires an existing store or website to integrate, more complex setup.

5. Zazzle: Zazzle allows for a wider range of customizable products and is known for personalized items such as invitations, clothing, and home goods. Artists can upload designs, and customers can personalize certain products before purchasing.

- **Pros:** Extensive product range, allows for product personalization.
- **Cons:** Smaller art-specific audience compared to platforms like Society6 or Redbubble.

Best Practices for Using POD as an Artist

Simply uploading your work to a POD platform isn't enough to guarantee sales. You need a strategy to promote your products, maintain quality control, and engage your audience.

1. Select High-Quality Images: The quality of your images is critical for POD success. Ensure your artwork is scanned or photographed at high resolution to ensure it prints beautifully on all products. Most POD platforms recommend images that are at least 300 DPI (dots per inch) to avoid pixelation on larger items like prints or tapestries.

- **Tip:** Use professional photography or a high-quality scanner to capture your artwork. This is particularly important for textured or detailed pieces where the quality of the reproduction matters.

2. Optimize for Different Products: While your artwork may look great as a print, it might not translate well to other products, like phone cases or throw pillows. Take the time to preview how your designs look on different items, and adjust the placement, cropping, or background colors as needed.

- **Tip:** Many platforms allow you to customize how your design appears on each product. Use this feature to ensure your artwork looks its best across all items.

3. Pricing Your Products: POD platforms often allow

artists to set their own prices for prints and other items, while other product categories (like apparel or accessories) might have a fixed commission rate. Be strategic with your pricing, keeping in mind both your profit margins and what your audience is willing to pay.

- **Tip:** Consider offering tiered pricing for different product types (e.g., affordable prints and premium items like framed artwork or limited-edition pieces) to appeal to a broader audience.

4. Promote Your Products: Just because your products are available on a POD platform doesn't mean people will automatically find them. You'll need to actively promote your products through your website, social media, and email newsletters.

- **Tip:** Use social media platforms like Instagram and Pinterest to showcase how your artwork looks on different products. Consider running special promotions or discounts during peak shopping periods, like holidays.

5. Test and Review Product Quality: While POD platforms handle the production and shipping, it's a good idea to order samples of your own products to check the quality. This ensures that your customers are receiving items that meet your standards.

- **Tip:** Many platforms offer artist discounts on product samples, so take advantage of this to review the print quality, colors, and materials used in your products.

Diversifying Your POD Offerings

While many artists start with selling prints on POD platforms, you can expand your offerings by thinking creatively about what products might resonate with your audience. Some artists find success in niche product categories that reflect their personal style and appeal to specific markets.

1. Art Prints and Posters: Traditional prints are still a staple, but don't limit yourself to standard posters. Consider offering framed prints, canvas prints, or even metal prints to provide collectors with more options.

2. Home Decor: From pillows and blankets to wall tapestries, home decor items are a popular way for customers to incorporate your art into their living spaces. These items allow you to reach a broader audience, particularly those interested in interior design.

3. Apparel and Accessories: Many POD platforms offer customizable apparel such as T-shirts, hoodies, and tote bags. Think about how your artwork can translate to fashion items, and create designs that work well on clothing and accessories.

4. Stationery and Office Supplies: Items like notebooks, planners, and stickers are often overlooked but can appeal to a wide range of buyers, particularly students or professionals looking for unique desk accessories. If your art includes patterns, illustrations, or typography, these can work well on smaller items like stationery.

5. Limited Editions and Exclusives: To create a sense of urgency and exclusivity, consider offering limited-edition products or collaborating with another brand for special releases. This can encourage collectors to act quickly, knowing that only a limited number of items are available.

Maximizing Sales on POD Platforms

To truly capitalize on POD, you'll need to actively manage your online presence and engage with potential buyers. Here are some strategies to help you maximize your sales:

- **Leverage Seasonal Trends:** Create themed products that resonate with specific seasons, holidays, or events. For example, you could create holiday-themed prints or spring-inspired apparel collections.
- **Track Your Best-Selling Items:** Most POD platforms offer analytics tools that show which items are selling the most. Use this data to focus on promoting your most popular designs and expanding similar product lines.
- **Bundle Products:** Offering product bundles (such as a print and matching tote bag) can increase the perceived value and encourage customers to purchase multiple items.
- **Update Your Portfolio Regularly:** Keep your product offerings fresh by consistently uploading new

designs and collections. This keeps your audience engaged and encourages repeat purchases.

The Future of Print-on-Demand for Artists

As technology evolves, the potential for POD continues to grow. Some platforms are starting to incorporate eco-friendly materials, 3D printing, and augmented reality previews, allowing customers to better visualize how products will look in their space. Staying up-to-date with these trends can help you remain competitive and offer your audience the latest innovations in product customization.

Action Points

- Choose the right POD platform based on your goals and audience.
- Upload high-quality images optimized for various products.
- Strategically price your products to balance profit and affordability.
- Actively promote your POD offerings through social media and email marketing.
- Test product samples to ensure quality before offering them to customers.
- Keep your offerings fresh by regularly adding new designs and seasonal collections.

15

Licensing and Royalties

Licensing your art is one of the most effective ways to turn your creative output into a steady income stream. While selling original pieces or prints can provide direct sales, licensing allows you to earn ongoing revenue by granting others the right to use your artwork on products or in various media. It's an opportunity to reach broader markets while earning royalties for every product sold that features your work.

What Is Art Licensing?

Art licensing refers to the process of allowing a company or individual to use your artwork for specific purposes, usually in exchange for a royalty fee. You retain ownership of your artwork, but the licensee (the person or company licensing your work) has the right to reproduce it on products like clothing, home decor, stationery, or even in advertising. Licensing gives you access to multiple income streams without having to sell your original work outright, and it can open up new audiences for your art.

There are many industries that rely heavily on licensed artwork. Some of the most popular categories for art licensing include:

- **Home decor**: Art used on wallpaper, throw pillows, bed linens, or wall art.
- **Apparel**: Designs printed on clothing, such as T-shirts, scarves, and shoes.
- **Stationery**: Notebooks, planners, greeting cards, and other paper products.
- **Tech accessories**: Cases for phones, laptops, and tablets.
- **Textiles**: Fabric designs for upholstery, fashion, or interior decor.

The beauty of licensing is that your art can be reproduced across various products and markets, giving you the opportunity to reach a much broader audience than if you only sold physical pieces. In turn, each licensed product can earn you royalties, providing a passive income stream as the products continue to sell.

Understanding Licensing Agreements

When you enter into a licensing agreement, you're essentially granting a licensee the right to use your art for specific purposes. However, the details of that agreement can vary widely, depending on the type of license, the terms of the agreement, and the industry you're working in. Understanding these agreements and their legal implications is critical to ensuring you are properly compensated for your work.

Here are some key components of a typical art licensing agreement:

- **Exclusive vs. Non-Exclusive**: An exclusive agreement means you grant the licensee the sole right to use your artwork for a certain purpose within a certain market. A non-exclusive agreement allows you to license the same artwork to multiple companies simultaneously. Non-exclusive licenses generally give you more flexibility, while exclusive agreements often come with higher royalty rates.
- **Territory**: This specifies the geographic area where the licensee is allowed to sell products featuring your artwork. It could be a single country or region, or it could cover global sales.
- **Term**: The length of time the license is active. This could range from a few months to several years, depending on the agreement.
- **Royalty Rates**: Royalties are typically paid as a percentage of sales. The industry standard royalty rate for art licensing ranges from 5% to 15%, though it can vary

depending on the product category, the company, and the artist's reputation. Some agreements may include an advance on royalties—an upfront payment that's deducted from future royalty earnings.

- **Rights of Use**: This details exactly how the licensee can use your artwork. For example, can they alter or modify it? Are there restrictions on how it's reproduced? This section helps you retain control over your art while ensuring the licensee's rights are clearly defined.

Legal Aspects of Licensing Agreements

Understanding the legal intricacies of licensing agreements is crucial for protecting your rights as an artist. Licensing contracts can be complex, and a poorly worded agreement could leave you under-compensated or stripped of control over your work. Here are some key legal considerations to keep in mind when entering into a licensing deal:

- **Retain Copyright Ownership**: Ensure the contract clearly states that you retain the copyright to your artwork. Licensing grants usage rights, but it doesn't transfer ownership of the art itself. This allows you to retain control and license the same artwork to other companies (in non-exclusive deals) or use it in future projects.
- **Moral Rights**: In some countries, artists have "moral

rights" that allow them to prevent their work from being distorted or used in a way that damages their reputation. It's important to ensure that your licensing agreement respects these rights, particularly in international deals.

- **Payment Terms**: Be clear on how and when royalties will be paid. Will you receive quarterly or annual payments? Does the licensee provide royalty statements? Clarify whether there are any minimum sales thresholds that need to be met before you're paid.

- **Audit Clauses**: To protect yourself, consider including an audit clause that allows you to verify the licensee's sales figures. This ensures transparency in reporting and helps prevent underpayment.

Industry-Specific Licensing Strategies

Not all industries approach licensing in the same way. Understanding the specific needs and trends of different sectors can help you tailor your approach and increase your chances of landing lucrative deals. Here are a few industry-specific strategies for licensing your art:

- **Home Decor**: Home decor companies often look for large-scale designs and patterns that work well across textiles, wallpapers, and furniture. If your work lends itself to repeated patterns or has broad aesthetic appeal, you may find a good fit in this market. Consider showcasing your work in mockups to demonstrate how it can be applied to various products.

- **Apparel**: Licensing your artwork for clothing and accessories can be a great way to expand your brand's reach. Streetwear and fashion brands often look for bold, trendy designs that resonate with their audience. Keeping up with fashion trends and offering designs that reflect current styles can increase your chances of success in this industry.

- **Stationery**: The stationery market is always in demand for fresh, vibrant artwork, particularly for greeting cards, planners, and notebooks. The key to licensing in this sector is creating versatile designs that can be used for a variety of occasions (holidays, birthdays, etc.).

- **Tech Accessories**: Artists whose work appeals to tech-savvy audiences may find success licensing their designs for phone cases, laptop skins, and other tech accessories. Bold, graphic designs tend to do well in this space, as they help customers express their personal style through their devices.

Case Studies: Successful Art Licensing

Learning from successful artists who have built lucrative licensing careers can provide valuable insights into how to approach the process. Here are two case studies highlighting artists who have successfully leveraged licensing deals to expand their reach and income:

- **Lisa Congdon**: Lisa Congdon is a well-known artist and illustrator who has licensed her bold, colorful designs to a variety of products, including home goods, apparel, and stationery. Congdon credits her success to building a strong personal brand and being selective about which companies she partners with. By licensing her art to a diverse range of products, she has built a sustainable income stream that complements her original work and book deals.
- **Kelly Rae Roberts**: Mixed-media artist Kelly Rae Roberts turned her whimsical, inspirational art into a licensing empire. Her designs have been licensed to companies that produce everything from wall art to jewelry to greeting cards. Roberts focuses on choosing licensees whose values align with her own, ensuring that her work reaches audiences who resonate with her artistic voice.

Marketing Your Licensed Products

Licensing your art is only half the battle. Once your designs are in the hands of a licensee, it's important to market those products to ensure they reach your target audience and generate sales. Here are some strategies for marketing your licensed products:

- **Collaborate with the Licensee**: Work closely with the company licensing your art to develop marketing campaigns that align with both your brand and theirs.

Many companies have marketing departments that will handle promotions, but you can amplify their efforts by sharing the product with your audience through social media, email newsletters, and your website.

- **Leverage Social Media**: Use platforms like Instagram and Pinterest to showcase your licensed products in use. Share high-quality images of the items in real-world settings and tag the brand or retailer that's selling them. This cross-promotion benefits both you and the licensee and can lead to increased exposure.

- **Offer Exclusives**: If possible, negotiate with your licensee to offer exclusive products or designs through your own channels, such as your website or at events. This creates a sense of scarcity and can encourage more sales.

International Licensing

Licensing your art internationally can open up even more opportunities for revenue, but it also comes with unique challenges. Here's what to consider when exploring international licensing deals:

- **Cultural Considerations**: Not all artwork translates equally across different cultures. Before entering an international licensing deal, research the market to ensure your work will resonate with the target audience. Some colors, symbols, or themes may hold different meanings in other countries.

- **Legal Protection**: International licensing agreements need to account for different intellectual property laws in each country. Make sure your contract is legally binding in the regions where your art will be used, and consider consulting an intellectual property attorney who specializes in international deals.
- **Global Market Trends**: Be aware of trends in the global market that may impact the demand for your art. For example, certain styles of art may be more popular in Europe or Asia than in North America. Keep an eye on international design trends and tailor your licensing approach accordingly.

Action Points

- Research potential licensing partners in your target industries (home decor, apparel, stationery, etc.).
- Ensure that any licensing agreements you enter into protect your rights, including retaining copyright ownership.
- Work with an intellectual property lawyer to review contracts, especially for exclusive deals or international agreements.
- Negotiate royalty rates based on the industry standard, keeping in mind the value of your art and the scope of the agreement.
- Use mockups to show potential licensees how your art can be applied to different products, making it easier for them to visualize the commercial potential.

- Build strong relationships with your licensees to collaborate on marketing strategies that boost both parties' visibility and sales.
- Keep up with market trends to identify new opportunities for licensing, especially in growing industries like tech accessories or eco-friendly products.
- Use social media to promote your licensed products and build cross-promotion opportunities with the companies you partner with.
- Stay informed about the legal and cultural differences when licensing internationally, and make sure your contracts account for regional laws.

16

Legal Advice for Artists

T he world of art is rich with creativity, but it also comes with a set of legal complexities that every artist needs to navigate. Understanding the legal side of your art career is essential to protect your work, your rights, and your financial interests. Whether it's safeguarding your intellectual property, negotiating contracts, or understanding the implications of licensing and royalties, legal knowledge can give you peace of mind and confidence in your artistic practice.

Copyright: Protecting Your Work

At the heart of protecting your art lies copyright law. Copyright automatically grants the creator of original works—such as paintings, sculptures, digital art, and more—exclusive rights to reproduce, distribute, display, and sell their work. In most countries, you don't need to register your work to hold copyright; it is inherent from the moment your artwork is created.

However, registering your work with the appropriate copyright office (e.g., the U.S. Copyright Office) provides additional legal protections, especially if you ever need to enforce your rights through legal action. Copyright gives you control over how your work is used by others and allows you to license or sell those rights.

Key Tips for Protecting Copyright:

- **Document Your Work:** Keep detailed records of your creative process, including dated sketches, drafts, and photographs of the final piece. This can help prove ownership if your rights are ever challenged.
- **Consider Registration:** While copyright is automatic, registering your work strengthens your ability to claim damages in case of infringement.
- **Mark Your Work:** Clearly label your work with a copyright symbol (©), your name, and the date of creation. While not legally required, this can serve as a deterrent to potential infringers and shows that you're aware of your rights.

Licensing: Monetizing Your Work Legally

Licensing is an important revenue stream for many artists, allowing others to legally use your art for various purposes —while you retain ownership of the original work. In a licensing agreement, you grant permission to a licensee (such as a company or individual) to use your artwork on their products, in advertisements, or for other purposes in exchange for compensation.

There are different types of licensing agreements, including:

- **Exclusive Licensing:** You grant the licensee exclusive rights to use your work in a particular market or geographic region, meaning you can't license it to anyone else in that space.
- **Non-exclusive Licensing:** You retain the right to license your work to multiple parties, giving you more flexibility and potential for multiple income streams.
- **One-Time Use Licensing:** You allow the licensee to use your work for a specific, one-time purpose, such as for a magazine cover or a limited-edition product run.

Important Considerations for Licensing Agreements:

- **Scope of Use:** Specify how the licensee can use your artwork—whether it's for merchandise, branding, or other purposes. Be clear about the limits on reproduction, distribution, and geographic range.

- **Duration of the Agreement:** Define the length of the licensing period. Will the license last for six months, one year, or indefinitely?
- **Compensation:** Will you be paid a flat fee, royalties, or a combination of both? Make sure the terms of payment are clear.
- **Rights Reserved:** Specify which rights you're retaining, such as the ability to license the work for other uses, create derivative works, or sell the original.

Royalties: Creating Ongoing Revenue

Royalties provide a way for artists to earn ongoing income from the use of their work. When you license your art, royalties are typically a percentage of the revenue generated by the use of your artwork. For example, if a company licenses your art to use on T-shirts, you may earn a royalty for each item sold.

Royalty rates can vary depending on the type of product and the size of the licensee. In general, royalties range from 5% to 15% of the sale price, though they may be higher for high-demand artwork or larger agreements.

Factors That Affect Royalties:

- **Industry Standards:** Different industries have standard royalty rates. For example, artists licensing their work for textiles may receive different royalty rates compared to those licensing art for book covers or advertisements.

- **Exclusivity:** Exclusive licensing agreements often come with higher royalty rates because the licensee has exclusive rights to use the artwork within a specific context.

- **Sales Volume:** Some agreements include a sliding scale, where royalties increase as sales reach higher thresholds. For example, you might receive a higher percentage once sales exceed 10,000 units.

Contracts: Avoiding Disputes

Contracts are essential for defining the terms of any business relationship, from licensing agreements to commissions. Without a written contract, you leave yourself vulnerable to misunderstandings, unpaid fees, and legal disputes.

A good contract should be clear, specific, and thorough. It should outline what each party is expected to deliver, the timeline for completion, and the terms of payment. Contracts should also address issues like intellectual property rights, termination clauses, and how disputes will be resolved.

Elements to Include in Contracts:

- **Scope of Work:** Clearly outline what services or artwork you are providing. This can include details such as the size, medium, and style of the commissioned piece or the specific rights being licensed.

- **Payment Terms:** Specify how and when you'll be paid. Will there be an upfront deposit, milestone payments, or a lump sum upon delivery?
- **Copyright and Usage Rights:** Clarify whether you retain copyright ownership or transfer certain rights to the other party. Be explicit about what the other party can and cannot do with your artwork.
- **Delivery and Deadlines:** Establish deadlines for the completion of the work or the duration of the licensing agreement. Include provisions for extensions or late delivery.
- **Termination and Dispute Resolution:** Outline how either party can terminate the agreement and how disputes will be resolved (e.g., through mediation, arbitration, or litigation).

Protecting Your Intellectual Property

In addition to copyright, other forms of intellectual property protection may apply to your work. For example, you may want to trademark your artist name or logo if you're building a brand around your work. Trademarks protect symbols, names, and slogans that distinguish your art from others in the marketplace.

Types of Intellectual Property Protections:

- **Copyright:** Protects original works of art from being reproduced or distributed without permission.

- **Trademark:** Protects your brand identity, including your name, logo, or any distinctive mark associated with your art.
- **Trade Secret:** Protects confidential business information, such as unique techniques or processes that give you a competitive advantage.

Public Domain and Fair Use

Understanding public domain and fair use is also critical for artists, especially if you're incorporating other works into your creations. Public domain works are free to use because their copyright has expired or the creator has relinquished copyright. Fair use, on the other hand, allows for limited use of copyrighted material without permission under certain conditions, such as for commentary, criticism, or education.

If you're unsure whether a work is in the public domain or falls under fair use, it's essential to seek legal advice before using it.

International Considerations

If you sell or license your work internationally, be aware that copyright and intellectual property laws vary by country. Some countries may not have the same protections as others, so it's crucial to understand how your work will be protected abroad.

When entering into international agreements, consider

adding clauses that specify which country's laws will govern the contract and how disputes will be resolved across borders.

Action Points

- Register your artwork with the U.S. Copyright Office or the equivalent office in your country for stronger protection.
- Use clear, written contracts for all business agreements, especially for licensing, commissions, and royalties.
- Understand the terms of licensing agreements, including exclusivity, duration, and scope of use.
- Protect your intellectual property by exploring options like copyright, trademarks, and trade secrets.
- Stay informed about international copyright laws if you plan to sell or license your work abroad.

17

Technology and the New Media: Shaping the Future of Art

In today's art world, technology has become a cornerstone of how artists create, share, sell, and engage with audiences. The advent of digital platforms, new media tools, and emerging technologies has completely reshaped the landscape of art-making and marketing. For artists who want to thrive in this modern environment, understanding and utilizing technology is not optional—it's essential.

From creating digital art to building online galleries, artists have more opportunities than ever before to reach a global audience, expand their creative practice, and streamline the business side of their work.

Digital Art Creation: New Tools for the Modern Artist

The rise of digital tools has opened up new frontiers in art creation, allowing artists to experiment with styles, media, and techniques in ways that were unimaginable just a few years ago.

- **Digital Painting Software**: Programs like Adobe Photoshop, Procreate, and Krita have transformed how artists approach painting. These platforms simulate the texture and behavior of real-world media like oils, watercolors, or pastels, while offering the convenience of unlimited layers, brushes, and editing tools. Artists can experiment freely without the cost of physical materials. For instance, using Procreate on an iPad with an Apple Pencil gives a hands-on, tactile experience that feels like drawing on paper but with the flexibility of digital features.

   Tip: If you're transitioning from traditional media, start by creating hybrid works. For example, scan or photograph your physical artwork and use digital painting tools to enhance or modify them.

- **Vector Art and Illustration**: Programs like Adobe Illustrator or Affinity Designer offer a different approach to digital creation by focusing on scalable, vector-based artwork. This is especially useful for artists working on logos, prints, or designs that need to maintain their quality at various sizes. Graphic artists and illustrators frequently use vector tools to create clean, scalable designs for commercial purposes.

- **3D Art and Modeling**: With tools like Blender, Cinema 4D, and Autodesk Maya, 3D modeling is another exciting avenue for artists. These programs allow for the creation of sculptures, virtual objects, and environments that can be rendered into images, animations, or even 3D-printed physical objects. Artists who typically work in sculpture, for example, can now explore creating digital versions of their pieces for virtual exhibitions or as part of an augmented reality project.

  Hands-On Tip: Start by scanning or photographing one of your physical pieces and bring it into a 3D modeling program. Experiment with creating a digital version or adding interactive elements that viewers can manipulate in a virtual space.

Immersive Technologies: AR and VR in Art

Immersive technologies like augmented reality (AR) and virtual reality (VR) are providing new and innovative ways for artists to present their work. These platforms offer the ability to create fully interactive, immersive art experiences, either in a digital environment or through overlaying digital elements on the physical world.

- **Augmented Reality (AR)**: AR allows digital content to be overlaid onto the real world through devices like smartphones or tablets. For artists, AR can be a powerful tool for adding interactive elements to physical artworks. Imagine viewers holding their phone up to your painting and watching as the colors animate or new layers of imagery are revealed.

Practical Application: Use AR to provide additional content, such as behind-the-scenes videos, process explanations, or even hidden layers of your art. Platforms like Artivive and Adobe Aero make it easier for artists to create AR-enhanced pieces. AR apps can also help collectors visualize how your art would look in their space before making a purchase, providing an extra level of engagement during the buying process.

• **Virtual Reality (VR)**: VR creates entirely immersive environments that people can experience through headsets like the Oculus Rift or HTC Vive. Artists can use VR to create entire virtual galleries, allowing visitors from around the world to walk through exhibitions, interact with art, and even experience time-based or interactive media in a way that isn't possible in physical spaces.

How to Get Started: Experiment with free or low-cost VR platforms like Google Tilt Brush to explore creating art in a 3D space. Artists can create environments or sculptures that viewers can "walk around" or interact with. This can be particularly useful for large-scale works or installations that are difficult to exhibit in traditional galleries. If you're looking to showcase work on a large scale, platforms like Mozilla Hubs allow you to build VR galleries and invite visitors to experience your work from any location.

Tip: Even if you don't create directly in VR, consider using it as a way to exhibit or promote your existing physical work. Offering a virtual walkthrough of your studio or exhibitions via VR platforms could reach an entirely new audience of tech-savvy art enthusiasts.

NFTs and Blockchain: A Revolution in Art Sales

One of the most talked-about technological developments in the art world has been the rise of NFTs (Non-Fungible Tokens) and blockchain technology. NFTs offer a digital certificate of ownership for artwork, stored on a blockchain, and have created a new, decentralized marketplace for digital and physical art.

- **What are NFTs?** NFTs allow digital artists to "mint" their work as unique tokens on the blockchain, proving authenticity and ownership. This technology has gained massive traction, especially for digital art, enabling artists to sell digital files as limited editions or originals. Platforms like OpenSea, Rarible, and Foundation provide marketplaces for artists to sell these NFT artworks.

    Hands-On Approach: If you're a digital artist, NFTs provide an exciting way to monetize your work. Start by researching blockchain platforms and familiarize yourself with the process of creating (minting) and selling NFTs. You'll need a cryptocurrency wallet, typically one that supports Ethereum, and basic knowledge of blockchain technology.

- **Royalties with NFTs**: One of the key advantages of NFTs is the ability for artists to earn royalties on secondary sales. When a collector resells your work, you can receive a percentage of the sale, which is automatically enforced by the smart contract on the blockchain. This feature makes NFTs especially appealing to artists, as they can continue to benefit from the increasing value of their work over time.

  Practical Tip: Consider minting both digital and physical versions of your work as NFTs. If you create physical art, you can mint an NFT as a "digital twin" to accompany the original piece. This could open up new markets and appeal to collectors who are interested in both traditional and digital assets.

Artificial Intelligence (AI) in Art

Artificial intelligence is increasingly becoming a tool for both creating and marketing art. While some artists may see AI as a threat, others are embracing it as a collaborative tool that enhances creativity and opens up new possibilities.

- **AI-Assisted Art Creation**: AI platforms like Artbreeder or DeepDream allow artists to collaborate with algorithms to create new artworks. You provide the AI with inputs—such as a base image or specific style—and the software generates unique outputs. These tools can help spark new creative ideas or even generate entire bodies of work.

Tip: Use AI tools as part of your creative process. Feed sketches or incomplete works into an AI generator and see what it produces. You can then refine or manipulate these outputs to fit your vision, blending human creativity with machine learning.

- **AI for Marketing**: Beyond creation, AI can be a powerful tool for marketing. Platforms like Hootsuite or Buffer use AI to recommend the best times to post on social media, analyze audience behavior, and suggest types of content that are more likely to resonate with your followers. AI-powered tools like Jasper or ChatGPT can also assist in drafting blog posts, newsletters, or even social media captions, streamlining your marketing efforts.

Crowdfunding and Patronage: Empowering Artists through Technology

Crowdfunding platforms and digital patronage systems have democratized funding for artists, allowing creators to raise money directly from their audience to support new projects, exhibitions, or ongoing work.

- **Crowdfunding Platforms**: Kickstarter, Indiegogo,

and GoFundMe allow artists to raise funds for specific projects or exhibitions. If you have an ambitious project in mind, these platforms offer a way to pre-sell your work, fundraise for materials, or even cover the costs of mounting an exhibition.

Pro Tip: When launching a crowdfunding campaign, create a compelling video and clearly outline the rewards for backers. Offer exclusive perks like limited-edition prints, behind-the-scenes access, or custom commissions to encourage contributions. Most importantly, set realistic funding goals and deliver on your promises to maintain credibility.

- **Patreon and Subscription Models**: Patreon has emerged as a popular platform for artists to generate a consistent income by offering exclusive content, early access, or limited-edition work to monthly subscribers. Artists use Patreon to create a community of loyal supporters who value the behind-the-scenes process just as much as the finished product.

Practical Strategy: Set up different tiers on Patreon, offering various levels of engagement. For example, a low-cost tier might offer exclusive behind-the-scenes updates or early access to new work, while higher tiers could include private virtual studio tours or exclusive commissions.

Data-Driven Marketing: Analytics and Automation

The integration of technology into marketing has made it easier than ever to measure success and refine strategies based on hard data.

- **Analytics for Artists**: Tools like Google Analytics, Instagram Insights, and Facebook's Page Insights allow artists to track how visitors engage with their websites and social media posts. By analyzing this data, you can identify trends, see what types of content drive the most engagement, and tailor your marketing efforts accordingly.

  Tip: Regularly review your website and social media analytics to understand where your traffic comes from and what types of posts generate the most interaction. This can help you fine-tune your online presence and identify potential new markets or strategies.

- **Automation Tools**: Scheduling tools like Later, Hootsuite, or Buffer can automatically post your content at optimal times, saving you time and ensuring that you maintain a consistent social media presence. These platforms allow you to batch-create content, schedule it in advance, and analyze performance metrics—all from one central dashboard.

  Pro Tip: Use automation tools to experiment with posting at different times of day or across different platforms. By scheduling posts in advance, you can dedicate more time to creating art without sacrificing your marketing efforts.

Action Points

- Explore digital creation tools like Procreate, Blender, or Adobe Illustrator to expand your artistic practice into the digital realm.
- Integrate AR or VR into your work to create immersive, interactive experiences for your audience.
- Learn how to mint and sell NFTs, taking advantage of blockchain technology to create new revenue streams.
- Collaborate with AI tools for both art creation and marketing, using AI-generated content to enhance your practice.
- Use crowdfunding platforms to raise funds for specific projects and engage your community through platforms like Kickstarter or Patreon.
- Analyze your audience engagement using data from analytics tools to refine your marketing strategy.
- Automate your social media posting using scheduling tools like Buffer or Hootsuite to maintain a consistent online presence while focusing on your creative work.

18

Pricing Your Art

Pricing your artwork is one of the most critical decisions you'll make as an artist. It directly influences not only your sales but also how you are perceived in the art market. Set the price too high, and you risk alienating potential buyers; set it too low, and you undervalue your work and may make it harder to build a sustainable career. Getting the pricing right means striking a delicate balance between market expectations, the costs of creation, and your personal goals as an artist.

By following these strategies, you can build a sustainable pricing model that reflects both the tangible and intangible value of your work. This not only helps you grow your art business but also ensures that you're compensated fairly for your creativity and effort.

Understanding the Costs Behind Your Art

Before setting any prices, it's essential to understand your own costs. These include both direct and indirect expenses:

- **Materials**: Paints, canvases, brushes, clay, digital tools, and any other materials used in the production of your work.
- **Studio Space**: If you rent or maintain a studio, that cost should be factored into the pricing of your pieces.
- **Time**: Your time is valuable, and it should be compensated. Think about how many hours go into creating each work of art, from concept to completion.
- **Marketing Costs**: Don't forget to include expenses related to marketing your work, such as website maintenance, promotional materials, and gallery fees.
- **Overhead**: Utilities, transportation, and general living expenses should also be considered when pricing your work, as they are part of what allows you to continue creating.

For many artists, a simple formula to start with is:

(Materials + Time + Overhead) x 2 = Price

This is just a starting point and gives you a sense of how much you need to cover your costs while making a profit. However, this basic formula may not be suitable for every artist, and as your career progresses, your pricing will depend on other factors.

Pricing Strategies for Different Markets

As an artist, you may operate in various markets, from direct sales to galleries to online platforms. Each market can require a different pricing approach.

Gallery Pricing

If you're selling through galleries, they typically take a commission of 40–50%. You need to price your work accordingly to ensure you still make a profit. The key here is consistency. If you price your work at $1,500 through a gallery, the price should be the same on your website or in direct sales. Undercutting the gallery pricing devalues your work and damages relationships with galleries.

Online Platforms

Platforms like Etsy, Saatchi Art, and Artfinder are common for artists selling their work online. Prices on these platforms tend to be lower than in galleries due to the reduced overhead. However, you'll still want to maintain consistency in pricing across platforms. Always account for platform fees when setting prices online.

Art Fairs and Exhibitions

Art fairs offer direct access to buyers, allowing for more flexibility in pricing. Here, artists often negotiate more and can experiment with pricing to see what resonates with collectors. Having a range of prices at these events—from affordable prints to higher-priced originals—can help attract different types of buyers.

Private Commissions

Commissions are another avenue where pricing can vary. When pricing commissioned work, you'll need to consider the specific requirements of the client and the level of customization involved. Commissions often carry a premium, as they are bespoke pieces that require extra effort. Many artists charge anywhere from 25% to 50% above their regular pricing for commissioned works.

Adding Emotional and Intangible Value

Your work is more than the sum of its materials and time—it also carries emotional and intangible value. Art is subjective, and its value can be influenced by factors like your personal reputation, past achievements, or the social and cultural impact of your pieces.

- **Reputation**: If you've built a strong reputation or have been featured in prominent exhibitions, this increases the perceived value of your work. Buyers are willing to pay more for art from an artist who has established credibility in the market.

- **Cultural Relevance**: If your work addresses contemporary social or political issues, or if it aligns with current trends in the art world, this can also drive up its value.
- **Scarcity**: Limited editions or one-of-a-kind pieces are often priced higher due to their exclusivity.

It's essential to communicate this intangible value to your buyers. In many cases, people are purchasing not just the artwork itself but the story behind it and the emotional connection they feel to it.

Communicating Value to Buyers

One of the challenges artists face is justifying their prices to potential buyers. Whether you're selling at a gallery or directly through your website, being able to confidently explain why your artwork is priced at a certain level is crucial. This involves educating your audience about what goes into your work.

Consider including details such as:

- **The complexity of your technique**: Are you using materials or methods that are rare or particularly challenging? Explain that to your audience.
- **The time and effort involved**: Break down how long it takes to create a piece and what's involved in your creative process. Many buyers don't realize the hours of work that go into each piece.

- **Your artistic journey**: Share your artistic background, past exhibitions, or awards. Demonstrating your professional development helps justify higher pricing.

Handling Negotiation

Negotiating prices is part of the art business. Some buyers may try to haggle, particularly in art fairs or direct sales. It's important to approach negotiations with confidence and maintain the integrity of your pricing.

- **Set your bottom line**: Know the lowest price you're willing to accept and don't go below it. Remember, selling your work at too low a price can devalue it in the eyes of other buyers.
- **Offer small discounts**: If you feel comfortable negotiating, consider offering a small discount or additional value (e.g., free shipping or framing). Be mindful not to give away too much, as this can undercut your pricing strategy.
- **Bulk purchases**: If a collector is interested in purchasing multiple pieces, you can offer a discount for bulk buys. This is a common practice in the art world and can help foster long-term relationships with collectors.

Tracking Market Trends

The art market is dynamic, and pricing should evolve as trends change. Global economic shifts, evolving artistic styles, and the rise of new artistic media (such as digital art or NFTs) can all influence pricing. As an artist, it's essential to stay informed about these shifts and adjust your pricing strategy accordingly.

- **Art Auctions**: Keeping an eye on auction sales can give you a sense of what collectors are paying for works in your genre.
- **Art Market Reports**: Publications like ArtPrice or the annual Art Basel and UBS Art Market Report offer valuable insights into pricing trends.
- **Competitor Pricing**: It's helpful to periodically review how other artists in your niche are pricing their work. However, always ensure that your prices align with your specific skill level, reputation, and market.

Reputation and Longevity

As your career grows, so should your prices. If you're just starting out, you may need to price your work lower to build a collector base. However, as you gain more exposure, win awards, and participate in prominent exhibitions, your reputation will allow you to command higher prices.

- **Track Record**: Have you consistently sold your work at a particular price? If so, you can gradually increase your prices, especially if demand increases.
- **Awards and Achievements**: Winning an award,

being featured in a prestigious gallery, or getting press coverage are all reasons to increase your prices.

- **Repeat Buyers**: If collectors are returning to buy more of your work, this indicates a healthy demand, allowing you to raise your prices without losing momentum.

Pricing for Different Types of Buyers

Not all buyers are the same. Different types of collectors, designers, and galleries will have varying expectations about pricing.

- **Personal Collectors**: These buyers often purchase based on emotional connections to the work. Price according to the value they perceive in owning a piece that speaks to them.
- **Interior Designers**: Designers are looking for pieces to complement their clients' homes or businesses. They may have specific budget constraints but can be valuable clients for commissions or multiple purchases.
- **Corporate Buyers**: Corporate clients often have larger budgets and are willing to pay more for work that aligns with their brand or office aesthetics. Be prepared to price higher for corporate commissions.

Collaborations and Licensing

Beyond selling individual pieces, many artists engage in collaborations or licensing agreements. This is especially common for artists working in illustration, graphic design, or product development.

- **Collaborations**: When working with a brand or company, pricing should include not only the cost of the artwork itself but also the value of your time and expertise. Artists often charge a premium for brand collaborations, as these projects often involve higher visibility and greater exposure.
- **Licensing**: Licensing your work for use on products (such as apparel, home goods, or stationery) can generate passive income. Pricing for licensing deals depends on factors like exclusivity, length of use, and the scope of distribution. In most cases, artists receive a percentage of sales (typically between 5% and 10%).

Legal and Tax Implications

As your art business grows, it's important to consider the legal and tax implications of your pricing. Taxes, invoicing, and legal documentation can all affect how you price your work.

- **Sales Tax**: Depending on where you live, you may need to charge sales tax on your artwork. Be sure to research local tax laws and factor these costs into your pricing.
- **Invoices**: Create clear and professional invoices for

every sale. This helps establish credibility with buyers and keeps your financial records organized.

- **Legal Contracts**: For larger sales, commissions, or licensing deals, consider using a contract to outline the terms of the sale. This protects both you and the buyer and ensures clarity on payment terms, deadlines, and other details.

Tools for Managing Pricing and Tracking Trends

To stay organized and on top of your pricing strategy, consider using digital tools and software designed to help artists track their sales, inventory, and pricing history. Tools like Artwork Archive or Artlogic can provide useful data on how your work is selling, allowing you to refine your pricing over time.

Action Points

- Calculate your pricing using the formula (Materials + Time + Overhead) x 2, then adjust for market value.
- Keep your pricing consistent across galleries, online platforms, and direct sales.
- Factor in intangible value, such as your reputation and the emotional connection to your work.
- Communicate the value of your work by sharing your process, techniques, and personal journey with buyers.

- Develop negotiation strategies to handle price haggling without undercutting your pricing integrity.
- Stay informed about market trends and adjust your prices accordingly.
- Tailor your pricing to different types of buyers, such as personal collectors, interior designers, or corporate clients.
- Consider collaborations and licensing as additional income streams, and price them according to the scope of the project.
- Be mindful of the legal and tax implications of your sales and pricing.
- Use digital tools to track your sales history, inventory, and pricing trends to refine your strategy over time.

19

Artist Grants and Funding

S ecuring financial resources is a significant aspect of sustaining an artistic practice. Beyond selling work, artists often rely on grants, fellowships, crowdfunding, and residencies to support their careers, pursue ambitious projects, and grow their creative practice.

Grants and funding opportunities can play a crucial role in advancing your career as an artist, providing financial stability and creative freedom. By applying for the right grants and managing the funds responsibly, you can unlock new opportunities and focus on what matters most—your art.

Why Artist Grants and Funding Matter

Artist grants and other forms of funding provide much more than financial support—they offer creative freedom, professional development, and validation from the art world. Here are the key reasons artist grants and funding are crucial:

1. **Financial Relief and Stability**: One of the most immediate benefits is financial security. Many artists face financial instability, especially during the early stages of their careers. Grants provide a cushion, allowing you to focus on creative work without worrying about how to cover everyday expenses.

2. **Freedom to Experiment**: Grants often come with fewer strings attached than commercial sales or commissions, offering greater creative freedom. With financial support, artists can take risks, explore new media or themes, and develop projects that might not have immediate commercial value.

3. **Career Advancement and Visibility**: Being awarded a grant can enhance your credibility and visibility within the art community. It shows that your work has been vetted and approved by respected professionals, which can lead to further opportunities, including exhibitions, residencies, or gallery representation.

4. **Networking and Mentorship**: Many fellowships and grants are attached to larger organizations, residencies, or programs that include networking, mentorship, and

exposure to curators, critics, and other artists. This can open doors for future projects and collaborations.

5. **Project Realization**: For project-based grants, the funding is specifically targeted to help you realize a body of work or exhibition that might otherwise be beyond your financial reach. This allows you to bring large-scale or ambitious ideas to life that could elevate your profile and expand your practice.

Types of Artist Grants and Funding

Artists can access a wide range of grants and funding sources. Knowing the different types available helps you tailor your search and applications.

1. Project-Specific Grants

These grants are designed to fund a specific project, whether that's a new series of artworks, a public art installation, or a solo exhibition. To win project-based grants, you'll need to provide a clear outline of the project, including details about the concept, timeline, and budget.

- **Example**: The **National Endowment for the Arts (NEA)** offers project-specific grants to support artistic innovation and public engagement.

Tips for Applying: Be as specific as possible. Outline the project's impact on your career, the art community, or society.

Show how this grant will enable you to achieve something unique or important that wouldn't be possible otherwise.

2. General Support Grants

Unlike project-specific grants, general support grants provide funding without a strict focus on a particular project. These grants allow you to use the money as you see fit to advance your artistic career. They can fund anything from materials and studio rent to travel or personal expenses.

- **Example**: The **Pollock-Krasner Foundation** offers grants to artists working in painting, sculpture, and other visual arts, with the funds being available for general studio needs or living expenses.

Tips for Applying: Focus on your long-term goals and demonstrate how this funding will help you grow as an artist. Provide a comprehensive overview of your practice and articulate how the grant will give you the time, space, or resources you need.

3. Fellowships

Fellowships offer both financial support and prestige. They often include stipends, studio space, and sometimes additional benefits like exhibitions, publications, or public talks. Fellowships are typically awarded to artists who have shown dedication and promise in their field.

- **Example**: The **Guggenheim Fellowship** is one of the most prestigious fellowships, providing support to exceptional individuals working across various art forms.

Tips for Applying: Fellowships often focus on career development and artistic merit. Highlight your past achievements and clearly outline your future artistic goals. A strong portfolio of work and a clear sense of direction are key to securing a fellowship.

4. Residency Grants

Residencies offer artists the chance to live and work in a new environment, often providing studio space, accommodation, and a stipend. Residencies can last from a few weeks to several months and offer focused time for creation, research, and experimentation.

- **Example**: The **MacDowell Colony** offers fully funded residencies to artists in a secluded, supportive environment, providing uninterrupted time for work.

Tips for Applying: Focus on how the residency will influence or benefit your work. Discuss how the change of environment or access to resources will impact your creative process or expand your practice.

5. Crowdfunding and Community-Supported Grants

Crowdfunding platforms like Kickstarter, Patreon, and Go-FundMe offer a direct-to-audience approach for artists to raise funds for projects. Additionally, some community organizations provide micro-grants to support local artists or public art initiatives.

- **Example: Kickstarter** allows artists to fund specific projects by offering rewards (like limited-edition prints or behind-the-scenes access) to supporters.

Tips for Success: Offer compelling rewards that appeal to your backers and tell a story that resonates emotionally. Be clear about how the funds will be used and offer regular updates to keep supporters engaged.

Finding Artist Grants and Funding

To successfully secure funding, you must know where to look and how to approach the search. Here are the most effective strategies for finding artist grants:

1. Online Grant Databases

Numerous websites curate lists of grants, fellowships, and funding opportunities for artists. These databases often allow you to filter by discipline, region, and type of funding.

- **Examples:**
  - ○ **NYFA (New York Foundation for the Arts)**: A comprehensive list of grants, fellowships, and awards.
  - ○ **Res Artis**: A global database of artist residencies that frequently offer funding.

2. Local and Regional Arts Councils

Your city or region likely has arts councils or foundations that provide grants to artists working in specific geographic areas. These grants often focus on community engagement or public art.

- **Examples:** The **Chicago Department of Cultural Affairs and Special Events (DCASE)** offers grants to local artists for creative projects that engage the community.

3. Art Organizations and Foundations

Many private foundations and nonprofit organizations fund artists whose work aligns with their mission or values. These foundations may focus on particular art forms, demographic groups, or social causes.

- **Example:** The **Joan Mitchell Foundation** provides funding to painters and sculptors, particularly those facing financial hardship.

4. Networking and Word of Mouth

Networking with other artists, curators, and arts professionals can provide invaluable insights into grant opportunities. Attend gallery openings, join artist groups, and participate in online forums where funding opportunities are shared.

Applying for Grants: A Step-by-Step Approach

Writing a strong grant application can make or break your chances of receiving funding. Here's a step-by-step guide to ensure your application stands out:

1. Research Thoroughly

Before applying, make sure you understand the grant's objectives and eligibility criteria. Tailor your application to show how your work aligns with the organization's mission.

2. Craft a Strong Proposal

Most grant applications require a written proposal that outlines your project's goals, timeline, and impact.

- **Articulate Your Vision**: Be clear about your project's artistic goals. What do you hope to accomplish, and why is this project important now?
- **Provide a Detailed Budget**: Show that you have

thought through the financial aspects of your project by providing a detailed and realistic budget.

- **Be Specific**: Avoid vague language. Specify how the funding will support your project, from purchasing materials to funding exhibition costs.

3. Prepare a Strong Portfolio

Your portfolio is your chance to showcase your artistic talent. Include high-quality images of your work, and if relevant, a short description of each piece or series.

- **Image Quality**: Submit clear, professional images that represent your work in the best possible light.
- **Contextualization**: For each piece, explain how it fits within your artistic practice or project proposal.

4. Write a Compelling Artist Statement

An artist statement should complement your portfolio, explaining the themes and ideas behind your work. This is an opportunity to give context to your creative practice and engage the reviewers on a deeper level.

Managing Your Grant Once Awarded

Receiving a grant is a major achievement, but managing the funds and fulfilling any obligations is equally important to maintain your reputation and set yourself up for future opportunities.

1. Develop a Budget and Spending Plan

Stick to the budget you outlined in your application. If unexpected expenses arise, adjust the budget thoughtfully to avoid running out of funds mid-project.

2. Track All Expenses

Most grant providers require financial reports or updates. Keep detailed records of how the money is spent, including receipts and invoices, to make reporting straightforward.

3. Maintain Communication

Keep your funders updated about your progress, especially if the grant requires regular reports. Open communication builds a positive relationship with grant providers and increases the likelihood of future funding.

4. Deliver on Your Promises

If your grant was tied to a specific project, make sure you meet the outlined goals and deadlines. If you experience setbacks, communicate these promptly and offer solutions.

Action Points

- Research and identify grants that align with your artistic practice and goals.
- Thoroughly read grant guidelines before applying to ensure eligibility.
- Craft a strong proposal that includes a detailed budget and timeline.
- Tailor your artist statement to connect emotionally with the grant reviewers.
- Submit a professional portfolio with high-quality images.
- Keep accurate records and adhere to grant reporting requirements.
- Develop strong relationships with grant providers for future funding opportunities.
- Explore non-traditional funding sources like crowdfunding and community grants.

20

Managing Sales and
Your Time Effectively

As an artist, you wear many hats. Beyond your creative practice, you must also run a business—managing sales, handling finances, promoting your work, and building relationships with clients. Balancing your artistic work with the business side can be challenging, but with the right strategies, you can effectively manage both your sales process and your time, ensuring you maintain creative flow while growing a sustainable art practice.

By mastering time management and streamlining your sales process, you'll be able to maintain a balance between your art and business, reducing stress and increasing productivity. These strategies will help you stay organized, meet deadlines, and continue building a successful art career.

Why Time Management is Essential for Artists

For artists, time is a non-renewable resource. Every hour spent managing the administrative side of your art business is an hour that could have been used for creation. As your career grows, it's easy to become overwhelmed by the sheer volume of tasks you need to handle—email inquiries, social media posts, shipping logistics, marketing, client follow-ups, and more. Without a system to manage these tasks efficiently, you risk burnout or stalling your creative progress.

Effective time management is about making deliberate choices with your time. It allows you to:

- Prioritize tasks that drive your career forward.
- Avoid getting bogged down by low-value activities.
- Create dedicated time for art, ensuring your creativity isn't compromised by administrative duties.

Many artists find themselves frustrated by the balance between the two, but it's important to remember that both creative and business tasks are crucial to long-term success. The key lies in learning how to manage your time and resources effectively so you can focus on the tasks that will have the most impact.

Structuring Your Days for Maximum Efficiency

A structured day is a productive day. By setting up a clear, organized schedule, you can ensure that you're dedicating enough time to both creating art and managing your business. A lack of structure often leads to procrastination or stress, particularly when faced with pressing deadlines or competing demands.

Time Blocking for Artists

One highly effective strategy for structuring your day is time blocking, where you break your day into distinct blocks of time dedicated to specific tasks. For instance, you could allocate mornings for studio work, afternoons for business tasks like sales and marketing, and evenings for personal time. The key is to remain consistent with this schedule, ensuring you don't allow business tasks to eat into your creative hours or vice versa.

Example:

- **9 a.m. – 1 p.m.:** Studio time (creating art, working on commissions)
- **1 p.m. – 2 p.m.:** Lunch break

- **2 p.m. – 5 p.m.:** Administrative tasks (emailing clients, processing sales, shipping)
- **5 p.m. – 6 p.m.:** Social media updates and marketing
- **6 p.m. onward:** Personal time or additional studio work

This type of structure gives each activity a clear time slot, ensuring nothing gets neglected, while still allowing you to focus on your art.

Prioritization Techniques

To avoid feeling overwhelmed by a long to-do list, it's essential to prioritize tasks. Not all activities carry the same weight. Some tasks are high-value, meaning they directly contribute to your artistic career's growth (e.g., working on a new piece for a major exhibition or responding to a collector inquiry). Others, while necessary, might not drive the same immediate results (e.g., reorganizing your studio or updating your website).

A helpful tool for prioritizing tasks is the **Eisenhower Matrix**, which divides tasks into four quadrants:

1. **Urgent and Important:** Tasks that need immediate attention (e.g., meeting a commission deadline or processing a sale).
2. **Important but Not Urgent:** Tasks that contribute to long-term goals but aren't time-sensitive (e.g., developing a new series or applying to art competitions).

3. **Urgent but Not Important:** Tasks that need attention soon but don't significantly impact your career (e.g., non-critical emails or routine tasks).

4. **Not Urgent and Not Important:** Tasks that don't add significant value (e.g., excessive social media browsing).

By prioritizing tasks in this way, you can ensure you're spending your time on what matters most.

THE EISENHOWER MATRIX

	URGENT	NOT URGENT
IMPORTANT	DO	DECIDE
NOT IMPORTANT	DELEGATE	DELETE

Streamlining Your Sales Process

Sales management is critical for an artist's career, but it can become overwhelming, especially when you're juggling multiple projects or platforms. By streamlining your sales process, you can make it more efficient, freeing up time to focus on your art.

Setting Up Your Sales Infrastructure

If you primarily sell art online, having a robust, user-friendly system in place is essential for managing sales smoothly. Whether you sell through your own website or use platforms like Etsy, Shopify, or Squarespace, automating key aspects of your sales process can save you time and reduce stress.

E-Commerce Solutions

A high-functioning e-commerce system allows you to:

- List artwork for sale quickly and easily.
- Automatically process payments through secure gateways.
- Track sales and inventory in real-time.
- Generate shipping labels and track shipments without manual input.

Consider using a platform that integrates these features, such as Shopify, Big Cartel, or Etsy, so that you can manage all aspects of a sale from one dashboard. Automating payments and shipping details can significantly reduce the time spent on logistical tasks and improve the customer experience.

Direct Sales Through Email or Social Media

For larger or custom pieces, many artists prefer handling sales through direct contact with buyers—whether through social media direct messages (DMs), email, or in-person discussions. However, managing direct sales can become time-consuming without a clear system in place.

Here's how to streamline this process:

- **Pre-written Responses**: Prepare standard responses for common inquiries, such as pricing, shipping costs, and availability. You can customize these templates slightly for each inquiry, saving time while maintaining a personal touch.
- **Clear Policies**: Develop clear sales policies that outline payment methods, timelines for delivery, and returns (if applicable). Display these prominently on your website or share them via email when a buyer inquires.
- **Payment and Invoicing**: Use tools like PayPal, Venmo, or Stripe to manage payments securely and efficiently. These platforms offer invoicing features that make it easy to track and manage transactions.

Managing Orders and Shipping

Shipping artwork can be complicated, especially for larger pieces or international orders. Developing an organized shipping process is crucial to ensuring your customers receive their purchases in a timely and professional manner.

Key tips for managing shipping:

- **Pre-Set Shipping Costs**: Many e-commerce platforms allow you to integrate real-time shipping rates from carriers like USPS, FedEx, or UPS. This automates shipping cost calculations, ensuring you don't need to manually estimate or undercharge for shipping.
- **Packaging**: Invest in high-quality packing materials, especially for fragile items like paintings or sculptures. Make sure your artwork is securely packaged and labeled appropriately. Having a standard packing procedure in place can streamline the process and reduce the risk of damage in transit.
- **Shipping Software**: Use shipping software like ShipStation or Pirate Ship, which allows you to automate the label creation process and track shipments. These tools often offer discounted shipping rates and help you manage multiple carriers in one place.
- **International Shipping**: International orders require special attention. Ensure you're aware of customs regulations and duties for shipping to different countries. Provide clear information to international buyers about potential customs fees or delays.

Balancing Sales with Studio Time

One of the biggest challenges for artists is finding a balance between sales and creative time. While making sales is essential for sustaining your business, overcommitting to administrative tasks can leave you drained and with little time or energy for creative work.

Batch Processing Business Tasks

One effective strategy for minimizing the impact of sales tasks on your studio time is batching. Instead of handling inquiries, payments, and shipping on a rolling basis throughout the day, set aside dedicated blocks of time to batch process these tasks. For example, you might dedicate two afternoons a week solely to processing orders, managing inquiries, and handling administrative tasks.

Batching reduces the time lost to constant task-switching and allows you to focus fully on creating during your designated art time.

Set Boundaries for Studio and Sales Work

Establish boundaries for when you'll focus on sales and when you'll focus on art. This might involve setting specific "office hours" for when you respond to customer inquiries or handle sales tasks, leaving the rest of your time for creating. Communicate these boundaries to your clients—for example, let them know they can expect responses within 24 hours during business hours, but that you dedicate certain times to studio work.

Tracking Sales and Payments

Managing your sales effectively also means keeping track of financial data. This includes not just recording payments and invoicing clients but also tracking expenses, taxes, and profits.

Accounting Software and Tools

Using accounting software like QuickBooks, Xero, or Wave allows you to automate invoicing, manage payments, and track your finances in real-time. These tools offer a simple, streamlined way to ensure you're staying on top of your financial records, which is critical during tax season or when planning for your business's future growth.

Financial Reports

Set a regular schedule—whether weekly, monthly, or quarterly—to review your financial reports. Pay attention to metrics such as:

- **Total Sales**: Track how much revenue you've generated from sales, including breakdowns by product type or platform.
- **Expenses**: Monitor business expenses, including supplies, shipping, and marketing costs. This helps you maintain a clear understanding of your profit margins.
- **Cash Flow**: Keep an eye on cash flow, particularly during slower sales periods. Ensuring that you have sufficient funds to cover ongoing expenses is key to maintaining a healthy business.
- **Tax Obligations**: Stay aware of your tax obligations, including sales tax and income tax, especially if you're selling across multiple states or internationally.

Using Technology to Manage Your Time and Sales

Digital tools can make a significant difference in how efficiently you manage your time and sales. There are a variety of tools that can help you organize tasks, track time, and ensure you're maximizing productivity.

1. Task Management Tools

- **Trello**: A simple, intuitive tool that allows you to create boards, lists, and cards to organize tasks. It's an excellent way to track deadlines, organize commissions, and visualize your progress.
- **Asana**: Similar to Trello, Asana helps you manage projects, set goals, and assign tasks. This is particularly useful if you work with assistants or collaborators, as you can delegate tasks easily.

2. Time-Tracking Apps

- **Toggl**: A time-tracking tool that helps you see how much time you're spending on different activities. It's a great way to identify time-wasting activities and ensure that you're dedicating enough time to both creating art and managing sales.
- **RescueTime**: This app helps you track how much time you spend on websites, social media, and other online activities. By reviewing your usage, you can adjust your habits and ensure that you're staying productive.

3. *Digital Calendars*

- **Google Calendar**: Using a digital calendar can help you manage your schedule and keep track of important deadlines. You can set reminders, share your calendar with collaborators, and block out time for both creative and business tasks.

Action Points

- Use time-blocking techniques to structure your day and create dedicated hours for art creation and business management.
- Set up an efficient e-commerce system that automates payments, shipping, and inventory tracking to streamline your sales process.
- Create templates for responding to common sales inquiries, allowing you to communicate efficiently without sacrificing personal touch.
- Use task management tools like Trello or Asana to stay organized and keep track of deadlines, commissions, and ongoing projects.
- Batch similar tasks together to minimize distractions and improve focus on both business and creative work.
- Track sales and payments through accounting software or spreadsheets to ensure that you stay on top of your financials and avoid any mistakes.
- Prioritize high-value tasks that contribute directly to your long-term goals, and delegate or automate low-value tasks whenever possible.

21

Tracking and Improving Your Marketing Efforts

Marketing is not a one-size-fits-all endeavor. Every artist's audience is different, and what works for one person may not work for another. This is why tracking your marketing efforts is so important—it allows you to tailor your strategy to your unique audience and needs.

By tracking key metrics, you can:

- **Identify which channels are most effective** at driving traffic to your website or online store.
- **Discover what type of content resonates most** with your audience.

- **Optimize your marketing spend** to ensure you're getting the best return on investment (ROI).
- **Spot opportunities for growth** by analyzing trends in your followers, engagement, and sales.
- **Improve your marketing strategy over time** by learning from your successes and failures.

Setting Measurable Goals

Before you can start tracking your marketing efforts, it's essential to set clear, measurable goals. These goals should be specific, attainable, and relevant to your overall objectives as an artist. For example:

- **Increase website traffic by 20%** in the next three months.
- **Grow your email list by 200 subscribers** in the next six months.
- **Sell 15 pieces of art** through Instagram by the end of the year.
- **Increase engagement (likes, shares, comments) on social media** by 10% over the next month.

Each goal should be paired with a metric that you can track to measure your progress. This will help you stay focused and allow you to see the direct impact of your marketing efforts.

Key Marketing Metrics to Track

The success of your marketing strategy hinges on identifying and measuring the right metrics. Here are the key performance indicators (KPIs) you should monitor:

Website Traffic

Tracking the number of visitors to your website is one of the most straightforward ways to measure your online presence. You can use tools like **Google Analytics** to see how many people are visiting your site, which pages they're viewing, and how long they're staying.

Key metrics to monitor:

- **Total website visits**: This gives you a broad view of how much traffic your site is generating.
- **Traffic sources**: This tells you where your visitors are coming from (e.g., social media, search engines, email marketing, or referrals from other websites).
- **Bounce rate**: This measures how many visitors leave your site after viewing only one page. A high bounce rate may indicate that visitors aren't finding what they're looking for or that your site isn't engaging them.
- **Average session duration**: The amount of time visitors spend on your site, which can signal how interested they are in your content.

Social Media Engagement

Social media platforms like Instagram, Facebook, and Tik-Tok are critical for building a following and engaging with your audience. Tracking social media engagement helps you understand how well your content resonates with your followers.

Key metrics to track:

- **Follower growth**: The number of new followers you're gaining over time. A steady increase shows that your content is attracting new people.
- **Likes, shares, and comments**: These indicate how much engagement your posts are generating. Posts with higher engagement are more likely to be shown to a broader audience by social media algorithms.
- **Post reach and impressions**: Reach measures how many people see your content, while impressions track the number of times your content is displayed. These metrics help you understand how far your content is spreading.
- **Engagement rate**: This is the percentage of people who engage with your posts compared to the number of people who saw them. A high engagement rate shows that your content is resonating with your audience.

Email Marketing Performance

Email newsletters are a powerful tool for building a direct connection with your audience. To ensure your email marketing efforts are effective, track how well your emails are performing.

Key metrics to track:

- **Open rate**: The percentage of recipients who open your emails. A higher open rate indicates that your subject lines are compelling and that your audience is interested in what you have to say.
- **Click-through rate (CTR)**: The percentage of people who click on a link in your email. A high CTR suggests that your email content is engaging and that your calls to action are effective.
- **Unsubscribe rate**: The percentage of recipients who unsubscribe from your emails after receiving a message. A low unsubscribe rate means that your content is valuable and relevant to your audience.

Sales and Conversions

At the end of the day, your goal as an artist is to sell your work. Tracking sales and conversions is critical for understanding how effective your marketing efforts are at driving revenue.

Key metrics to track:

- **Total sales**: The number of artworks or products you've sold. Monitor how this number changes over time and in response to specific marketing campaigns.
- **Conversion rate**: The percentage of website visitors

who make a purchase. A higher conversion rate means that your site is doing a good job of turning visitors into buyers.

- **Average order value**: The average amount of money customers spend when they make a purchase. Tracking this can help you identify opportunities to upsell or offer bundles to increase the value of each sale.

Customer Retention

Building a loyal customer base is key to long-term success. It's much easier (and more cost-effective) to sell to existing customers than to acquire new ones. Measuring customer retention helps you understand how well you're nurturing your relationships with buyers.

Key metrics to track:

- **Repeat purchase rate**: The percentage of customers who return to buy from you again. A high repeat purchase rate suggests that you're doing a good job of building relationships and providing value to your customers.
- **Customer lifetime value (CLV)**: The total revenue you can expect to generate from a single customer over the duration of your relationship with them. A higher CLV indicates that your marketing efforts are not only attracting buyers but keeping them engaged over the long term.

Tools for Tracking Marketing Efforts

There are several tools available to help you track and analyze your marketing performance. These tools provide detailed insights into your data and make it easier to identify trends and areas for improvement.

1. **Google Analytics**: Essential for tracking website traffic, user behavior, and conversions. Google Analytics provides a comprehensive overview of how visitors interact with your website and which marketing channels are driving the most traffic.

2. **Instagram Insights**: Built directly into the Instagram app, this tool allows you to track engagement, reach, impressions, and follower growth for your posts, stories, and reels.

3. **Facebook Insights**: Similar to Instagram Insights, Facebook offers analytics for your business page, including data on likes, shares, post reach, and follower demographics.

4. **Mailchimp** (or similar email marketing platforms): Provides detailed analytics on email open rates, click-through rates, and subscriber growth.

5. **Hootsuite** or **Buffer**: Social media management tools that allow you to schedule posts, track engagement, and measure performance across multiple platforms.

6. **Google Search Console**: This tool helps you understand how your website is performing in Google search

results and how users are finding your site through search engines.

7. **E-commerce Platforms** (Shopify, Squarespace, etc.): Most online store platforms offer built-in analytics that track sales, conversion rates, and customer behavior on your site.

Improving Your Marketing Efforts

Once you've started tracking your marketing performance, it's time to use that data to make improvements. Here's how you can use your insights to optimize your strategy:

1. Refine Your Content Strategy

If you notice that certain types of content consistently perform better than others, focus on producing more of that. For example, if your behind-the-scenes videos or process photos generate more engagement than static images of your finished work, incorporate more of that content into your social media plan. Use A/B testing for email subject lines or social media posts to see which ones resonate more with your audience.

2. Adjust Your Posting Schedule

Tracking when your audience is most active on social media or when your emails are most likely to be opened can help you fine-tune your posting schedule. Tools like Instagram

Insights show you the times of day your followers are most engaged, allowing you to post content when it's more likely to be seen.

3. Improve Your Website's User Experience

If your website has a high bounce rate, consider whether the design, navigation, or loading times are causing visitors to leave. Make your site easy to navigate with clear calls to action. Optimize for mobile users and ensure your portfolio is easily accessible. Regularly updating your site with new content also encourages visitors to return.

4. Revisit Your Pricing Strategy

If your conversion rate is low, it may be worth re-evaluating your pricing. Are you pricing your work too high for your audience? Alternatively, could you offer tiered pricing options, such as lower-cost prints alongside original works, to appeal to a wider range of buyers?

5. Enhance Your Email Marketing

If your open rates or click-through rates are lower than expected, consider experimenting with different email subject lines or formatting. Personalizing your emails, using storytelling, and providing value (such as exclusive discounts or behind-the-scenes content) can improve engagement.

6. Strengthen Customer Relationships

Encourage repeat business by nurturing relationships with your existing customers. Use email marketing to send personalized messages, offer exclusive previews of new work, or provide discounts to loyal buyers. Engaging with customers on social media and following up after sales with thank-you messages also helps build lasting connections.

Action Points

- **Set clear, measurable marketing goals** for your art business and align them with key performance indicators.
- **Track your website traffic** using tools like Google Analytics to understand how visitors interact with your site.
- **Monitor social media engagement** to see which types of content generate the most interest and interaction.
- **Use email marketing tools** to track open rates, click-through rates, and subscriber growth.
- **Measure sales performance** and conversion rates to ensure your marketing efforts are driving revenue.
- **Regularly analyze your data** and adjust your marketing strategies based on what works best.
- **Test new content types, posting schedules, and formats** to continually improve your marketing results.

22

Legal and Copyright Issues

As an artist, navigating the legal and copyright issues surrounding your work is crucial for protecting your rights and ensuring that you are properly compensated. From copyright law to contracts, licensing agreements, and protecting against infringement, understanding these legal issues will safeguard your creative output and help you avoid costly mistakes. Whether you are just starting out or have an established art practice, taking steps to protect your intellectual property is essential for maintaining control over how your art is used and distributed.

Copyright Law: The Foundation of Your Artistic Rights

At the core of legal protection for artists is copyright law. Copyright gives you the exclusive rights to your original works of art and allows you to control how your creations are used, shared, and reproduced. Unlike trademarks or patents, which need to be registered before protection takes effect, copyright automatically applies as soon as you create a tangible work. However, formally registering your copyright provides additional legal benefits.

What Copyright Protects

Copyright covers a wide range of artistic expressions, including:

- Paintings, drawings, and sculptures
- Photographs and digital art
- Graphic design and illustrations
- Installations, murals, and public art
- Video art and performance pieces

What Copyright Does Not Protect

- Ideas, concepts, or themes (you cannot copyright a style or general concept, only the specific work you create)
- Facts, processes, or systems (e.g., you can't copyright an art technique, but you can protect specific works created using that technique)

- Titles, slogans, or phrases

Registering Your Copyright

While your art is automatically protected by copyright law the moment it is created, registering it with the U.S. Copyright Office (or the relevant office in your country) provides additional legal benefits. Formal registration creates a public record of your ownership and gives you the right to sue for statutory damages and attorney's fees in cases of infringement.

To register your copyright, follow these steps:

1. Visit the U.S. Copyright Office website (or your country's equivalent).
2. Submit a completed application form.
3. Provide a copy or image of the work being registered.
4. Pay the registration fee (currently between $35 and $85 for most visual arts works in the U.S.).

Once registered, you will receive a copyright certificate, which offers legal evidence of your ownership.

International Copyright Protection

Copyright law varies by country, but many nations are signatories to international agreements like the **Berne Convention**, which ensures that artists' copyrights are respected across borders. As long as your country and the country where your art is being used are both members of the Berne Convention (most are), your copyright protection extends internationally.

However, enforcement of copyright laws can be more difficult internationally, especially in countries with weaker intellectual property regulations. It is advisable to consult with a legal professional experienced in international copyright issues if you plan to exhibit, sell, or license your art abroad.

Key Rights Under Copyright Law

Once you hold the copyright to your work, you have several exclusive rights, including:

1. **Reproduction**: Only you can create copies of your work.
2. **Distribution**: You control how your work is distributed—whether in print, online, or otherwise.
3. **Derivative Works**: You have the exclusive right to create adaptations or modifications of your work, such as turning a painting into a print series or using elements of a piece in new works.
4. **Public Display**: Only you can display your work publicly in galleries, online, or in public spaces.
5. **Performance**: For video or performance art, you have the right to control public performances of your work.

Moral Rights

In addition to economic rights, certain jurisdictions (including many European countries) also recognize **moral rights**. Moral rights include the right of attribution (ensuring that you are credited as the creator of your work) and the right of integrity (protecting your work from being altered in a way that damages its reputation or distorts your intention).

Licensing Your Art

Licensing allows you to generate income from your art while retaining ownership. By granting a license, you give someone else the right to use your work under specific conditions. Licensing is common in commercial and editorial contexts, such as when a company wants to use your art in advertising or when a publication wishes to feature your work.

Types of Licensing Agreements

1. **Exclusive License**: Grants the licensee sole rights to use your work for the agreed-upon purpose. This is often used for high-profile collaborations or large-scale commercial projects. Exclusive licenses typically command higher fees but limit your ability to license the work to others during the term of the agreement.
2. **Non-Exclusive License**: Allows you to license your work to multiple parties simultaneously. Non-exclusive licensing is common for print reproduction, digital

media, or merchandise, where the same artwork can be used across different platforms or products.

3. **Royalty-Free License**: A royalty-free license allows the licensee to use your work without paying ongoing royalties. Instead, they pay a one-time fee for indefinite use. This is common in stock photography and illustration markets.

Licensing Fees and Negotiation

When negotiating a licensing agreement, consider:

- **Upfront fees**: One-time payments for the use of your work.
- **Ongoing royalties**: Percentage-based payments, typically used for commercial products or continuous use (e.g., merchandise, book covers).
- **Duration of use**: Specify how long the license lasts—temporary licenses often come with renewal options.
- **Territory**: Define whether the license applies only to certain geographic regions or globally.
- **Exclusivity**: Decide whether the licensee has exclusive rights to your work or if you can license it to others.

Contracts: Safeguarding Your Rights

Contracts are crucial tools for formalizing agreements and protecting yourself from misunderstandings or disputes. Whether you are selling a piece, taking on a commission, or entering into a collaboration, contracts ensure that all parties are clear on the terms of the agreement.

Essential Elements of a Contract

For artists, a solid contract should include:

1. **Parties involved**: Clearly identify all individuals or organizations entering into the agreement.
2. **Description of the artwork**: Include detailed descriptions of the work being sold, licensed, or commissioned. For a commission, include specifications such as size, medium, and subject matter.
3. **Payment terms**: Specify how and when you will be paid, including deposits, payment milestones, and final payments.
4. **Rights granted**: For licensing agreements, clearly outline what rights are being granted (e.g., reproduction, distribution) and whether they are exclusive or non-exclusive.
5. **Delivery and deadlines**: If the contract involves commissioned work, include a timeline for completing the project.
6. **Termination and breach**: Specify under what conditions the contract can be terminated and what happens if one party fails to fulfill their obligations.
7. **Dispute resolution**: Outline how disputes will be handled—whether through mediation, arbitration, or legal proceedings.

Common Contracts for Artists

1. **Sales Contracts**: A simple contract between the artist and the buyer outlining the price, delivery terms, and transfer of ownership. It should also specify whether the buyer acquires full rights to the work or just the physical piece (in which case copyright remains with you).

2. **Commission Agreements**: For custom work, a commission contract clarifies what the client is requesting, the agreed-upon price, the timeline for completion, and how revisions or changes will be handled.

3. **Licensing Agreements**: When licensing your work for use in publications, products, or media, a licensing agreement should specify the scope of the license, including duration, territory, and exclusivity.

4. **Collaboration Agreements**: If you are working with another artist, designer, or company, a collaboration contract ensures that both parties understand their roles, contributions, and how profits or credit will be divided.

Protecting Your Work Against Infringement

Unfortunately, unauthorized use and reproduction of artwork are common in the digital age. From social media reposts to full-scale commercial infringements, it's important to know how to protect your work.

How to Respond to Infringement

1. **Document the infringement**: Gather as much evidence as possible, including screenshots, URLs, and physical copies of the infringing work.

2. **Cease-and-desist letter**: Often, the first step is to send a formal cease-and-desist letter demanding that the infringer stop using your work immediately. A lawyer can help draft this letter to increase its impact.

3. **Negotiation**: In some cases, the infringer may be willing to negotiate a settlement, such as offering compensation for unauthorized use.

4. **Legal action**: If the cease-and-desist letter and negotiation don't work, you may decide to pursue legal action. A copyright lawyer can help you file an infringement lawsuit in federal court, but keep in mind that litigation can often be costly and time-consuming. It may come down to weighing the costs against each other.

DMCA Takedown Notices

For online infringement, the **Digital Millennium Copyright Act (DMCA)** allows you to file takedown notices with websites hosting infringing content. Platforms like Instagram, YouTube, and Etsy have procedures for removing infringing content under the DMCA. This is a faster and less costly option than litigation.

Public Domain and Fair Use

Once copyright expires, works enter the **public domain** and are free for anyone to use without permission. In the U.S., copyright typically lasts for the artist's lifetime plus 70 years. Works created before 1924 are already in the public domain.

Fair use allows limited use of copyrighted works without permission, but this doctrine is complex and only applies in certain circumstances, such as criticism, commentary, or educational use. Always consult a lawyer if you believe fair use applies to your work or if someone claims it as a defense for using your art.

Action Points

- **Familiarize yourself** with the key aspects of copyright law, including your rights as an artist.
- **Register your work** with the U.S. Copyright Office (or your country's equivalent) to protect your work and enable legal action.
- **Draft and use contracts** for all sales, commissions, and licensing agreements to safeguard your interests and clarify terms.
- **Negotiate licensing agreements** carefully to ensure fair compensation and proper use of your work.
- **Monitor for infringement** online and in physical spaces, and take action promptly if your work is used without permission.
- **Explore international protections** if your work

is exhibited or sold abroad, and consider consulting an intellectual property lawyer with international expertise.

23

Final Thoughts and Next Steps

As you've journeyed through the chapters of this book, you've learned the essential building blocks of marketing your art effectively. By now, you understand that art marketing is much more than just promoting your latest works—it's about building a sustainable and authentic connection with your audience, establishing a solid brand, and continuously evolving to meet the changing demands of the market.

Art marketing is a long-term commitment that requires a mix of strategy, creativity, and consistency. Success doesn't happen overnight, but with patience and persistence, you can create a marketing plan that helps you thrive as an artist in today's competitive environment.

Recap of Key Concepts

1. **The Importance of Art Marketing**

   Art marketing is essential for getting your work noticed, building an audience, and creating opportunities for sales and collaborations. Whether you're just starting out or an established artist, having a clear marketing strategy allows you to take control of your career and reach collectors, galleries, and fans on your own terms.

2. **Building a Strong Foundation with a Business Plan**

   A solid business plan is the foundation for any successful art career. By defining your artistic goals and identifying your target audience, you give yourself a clear path to follow. Building a sustainable art practice requires setting achievable milestones, planning your finances, and managing your time effectively.

3. **Developing Your Personal Brand**

   Your brand is how you communicate your unique identity and vision as an artist. By developing a strong brand, you stand out in the crowded art world and create a lasting impression on your audience. Your brand should be consistent across all platforms, from your website and social media to the way you present yourself at exhibitions and events.

4. **Harnessing the Power of Social Media**

   Social media has become a game-changer for artists, providing a direct line to your audience. Platforms like Instagram, Facebook, and TikTok allow you to share your work in real time, engage with your followers, and sell directly to collectors. By creating an effective social media strategy, you can grow your audience, build engagement, and increase sales.

5. **Content Marketing Through Blogging and Email Newsletters**

Content marketing helps you build deeper relationships with your audience. Blogging allows you to share your creative process, inspirations, and expertise, while email newsletters offer a more personal way to keep your audience updated and engaged. Both tools are excellent for nurturing long-term relationships with collectors and fans.

6. **Navigating Online Art Markets and Print-on-Demand**

Online platforms have opened up new opportunities for artists to reach global audiences. Selling through online art markets, print-on-demand services, and your own website allows you to generate income beyond traditional galleries. Understanding how these platforms work and how to leverage them effectively is key to expanding your reach.

7. **Pricing Your Art and Managing Sales**

Pricing your art is one of the most challenging aspects of running an art business, but it's crucial for your long-term success. By developing a pricing strategy that reflects the value of your work, you can attract the right buyers and ensure that your business is profitable. Managing sales—whether online, in-person, or through galleries—requires organization, attention to detail, and clear communication with buyers.

8. **Tracking and Improving Your Marketing Efforts**
Successful marketing is data-driven. By tracking your performance—whether it's website traffic, social media engagement, or sales conversions—you can see what's working and what's not. Regularly reviewing your marketing efforts allows you to make informed decisions and continuously improve your strategy.

9. **Exploring Multiple Income Streams**
Diversifying your income is essential for financial stability as an artist. Whether through print sales, licensing, teaching, or commissions, having multiple income streams ensures that your business can weather market fluctuations and gives you the flexibility to focus on your creative practice.

Long-Term Success in Art Marketing

As you move forward in your art career, remember that marketing is an ongoing process that requires adaptability, creativity, and commitment. The art world is constantly changing—new platforms emerge, trends evolve, and audiences shift. The key to long-term success in art marketing is your ability to stay flexible and open to learning new strategies, while staying true to your artistic vision.

Consistency is Key

The most successful artists don't just market their work occasionally; they do it consistently. This means regularly updating your website, staying active on social media, maintaining your email newsletter, and continuously engaging with your audience. Consistent marketing builds trust and keeps your work top of mind for potential buyers and collaborators.

Be Open to Experimentation

Art marketing is not an exact science. What works for one artist may not work for another, and what works today might not work tomorrow. Don't be afraid to experiment with new platforms, content formats, or marketing techniques. Pay attention to trends, but also be willing to try unconventional approaches that reflect your unique style.

Build and Nurture Relationships

In the art world, relationships are everything. Whether it's with collectors, galleries, other artists, or influencers, the relationships you build can lead to new opportunities, collaborations, and sales. Always prioritize nurturing these connections by engaging with your audience, showing appreciation for your supporters, and seeking out meaningful partnerships.

Embrace Technology and Innovation

The digital landscape is constantly evolving, and staying ahead of the curve can give you a competitive edge. From augmented reality (AR) and virtual reality (VR) exhibitions to using AI tools to streamline your marketing efforts, technology offers new ways to present your art and reach your audience. Stay curious and embrace innovative tools that can help you expand your reach and enhance your marketing strategy.

Stay True to Your Vision

In the rush to market your work and grow your audience, it can be easy to lose sight of your artistic vision. Always remember that your creativity and authenticity are what make your work unique. While it's important to be strategic about your marketing, never compromise your vision for the sake of trends or quick sales. Stay true to your voice as an artist, and let your marketing efforts reflect that authenticity.

Final Words

Remember, your journey as an artist is unique. There's no one-size-fits-all approach to art marketing. What matters most is that you continue to push forward, stay adaptable, and, most importantly, stay true to your artistic vision. Your art has the power to connect with people in ways only you can create. Keep sharing your voice with the world, and success will follow.

About the Author

Evan Stuart Marshall is an award-winning mixed-media abstract artist, celebrated for his quirky, playful, and whimsical style. Originally from Boston and raised in Sharon, Massachusetts, he now lives and works in Roseland, New Jersey.

A largely self-taught artist, Evan has earned numerous accolades for his vibrant, distinctive paintings, which have been featured in solo and group exhibitions worldwide. His work, inspired by his love of color and texture, is held in private collections across the globe. His art is available through major online retailers including 1stDibs, Artsy, Wayfair, and Walmart, among others.

In addition to *Building Your Art Business*, Evan is the

author of *Abstract Art Revolution* and *Collecting Abstract Art on a Budget*.

Visit Evan's website at www.evanstuartmarshall.com.

Stay connected and follow his artistic journey on social media!

Facebook: facebook.com/evanstuartmarshall

Instagram: instagram.com/evanstuartmarshall

YouTube: youtube.com/evanstuartmarshallabstractart

Pinterest: pinterest.com/evanstuartmarshallart

X (formerly Twitter): x.com/esmarshallart

Appendix: Practical Tools and Templates for Artists

T his appendix provides step-by-step templates and work-sheets to help you implement the strategies discussed in this book. These practical tools are designed to guide you through key areas such as pricing your art, building a social media strategy, creating a business plan, and more. Feel free to customize these templates to fit your unique practice and goals.

1. Business Plan Template for Artists

A well-structured business plan will help you set clear goals and outline how to achieve them. Use this template to build your plan.

Executive Summary

- Describe your art business in one or two sentences. What type of art do you create? What are your short- and long-term goals?

Artistic Goals

- Short-term goals (next 6-12 months)
- Long-term goals (next 2-5 years)

Target Audience

- Who are your ideal collectors or clients? Include demographics, geographic locations, and art preferences.

Revenue Streams

- List all possible income streams (e.g., original art sales, commissions, licensing, print-on-demand, workshops).

Marketing Plan

- Outline how you will market your work, including social media platforms, email newsletters, and online sales strategies.

Financial Plan

- Estimate your projected income, expenses, and profit margins over the next year.

2. Pricing Template for Artists

This worksheet will help you calculate the price of your artwork based on your costs, time, and desired profit margin.

Materials Cost

- List all materials used for a piece (e.g., canvas, paint, brushes).
  - Total cost: $_____

Time Spent

- Hours spent on the artwork: _____
- Hourly rate: $_____
  - Total time cost: $_____

Overhead Costs

- Include studio rent, utilities, shipping, website fees, etc.
  - Monthly overhead: $_____
  - Percentage allocated to each artwork: $_____

Profit Margin

- Desired profit margin: _____%

Final Price Calculation

- Total material + time cost + overhead cost = $_____
- Add profit margin: $_____
- Suggested sale price: $_____

3. Social Media Strategy Template

Use this template to build a cohesive social media strategy that helps you engage your audience and grow your online presence.

Goals

- What do you want to achieve with social media? (e.g., increase followers, drive website traffic, sell art)

Target Audience

- Define your audience. Who are you trying to reach? What platforms are they using?

Content Types

- Decide what content you'll share. (e.g., process videos, behind-the-scenes, artwork showcases, artist tips)

Platforms

- Identify the platforms you'll focus on (e.g., Instagram, TikTok, Pinterest, Facebook, LinkedIn).

Posting Schedule

- How often will you post?
  - Weekly: ___ times per week.
  - Monthly: ___ times per month.

Hashtags & Keywords

- List the top 10 relevant hashtags/keywords you will consistently use to increase visibility.

4. Email Marketing Template

This email marketing plan will help you develop a newsletter strategy to stay in touch with collectors and fans.

Email List Building

- How will you grow your list? (e.g., website sign-ups, social media promotions, exhibitions)
  - Current email subscribers: _____
  - Target growth in 6 months: _____

Content Plan

- Types of emails you'll send (e.g., new work announcements, behind-the-scenes stories, upcoming exhibitions)
- Frequency: Monthly/Quarterly/Bi-weekly

Call to Action

- What will you ask subscribers to do? (e.g., visit your website, shop, RSVP to an event)

Engagement Metrics

- Track open rates, click-through rates, and unsubscribe rates for continual improvement.

5. Gallery Outreach and Tracking Template

Use this template to keep track of the galleries you contact and your progress with them.

Gallery Name

- Gallery 1: _____
- Gallery 2: _____

Contact Person

- Name: _____
- Email: _____

Date of First Contact

- Sent portfolio on: / /_____

Follow-Up

- Date of follow-up email or call: / /_____
- Response/Next Steps: _____

Outcome

- Accepted, Pending, Not a fit, Next exhibition:
  _____

6. Licensing and Royalties Tracking Template

For artists earning royalties from licensing deals, this template helps track income from each agreement.

Licensing Agreement

- Artwork licensed: _____
- Licensee: _____

- License type: (e.g., exclusive, non-exclusive)
- Duration of agreement: _____
- Royalty percentage: _____%

Payment Schedule

- Payment dates: _____
- Amount: $_____
- Total royalties earned: $_____

7. Tracking and Improving Your Marketing Efforts

Track and refine your marketing strategies with this worksheet.

Key Metrics to Track

- Social media engagement (likes, comments, shares)
- Email open rates: ____%
- Website traffic: ____
- Sales generated from each channel: ____

What's Working?

- Best-performing posts or emails:

  _____

Areas for Improvement

- How can you improve or pivot? (e.g., try different content, increase email frequency)

These tools are designed to help you stay organized, focused, and successful as you grow your art business. Regularly update these templates to reflect your progress and changing goals. With these practical worksheets in hand, you'll have a clear path to managing your art career effectively.

Appendix: What Does Success Mean to You? (The Quiz)

As artists, we all have different visions of what success looks like. Some may be driven by financial goals, while others are motivated by recognition, community building, or personal fulfillment. This quiz is designed to help you reflect on your own goals and understand what kind of success matters most to you. By understanding your priorities, you can create a marketing and business strategy that aligns with your values and strengths.

Answer the following questions, tally your score, and discover what success means for you as an artist—and how you can move forward to achieve it!

The Quiz

1. **When you imagine yourself as a successful artist, what is most important to you?**

   a. Making a lot of money from my work (4 points)

   b. Getting recognition from galleries and critics (3 points)

c. Gaining a large following on social media (2 points)

d. Being able to create the art I love without worrying about others' opinions (1 point)

2. **Which of the following would make you feel the most accomplished?**

a. Selling out an exhibition (4 points)

b. Winning an art award (3 points)

c. Gaining 10,000 followers online (2 points)

d. Finishing a body of work that I'm proud of (1 point)

3. **How do you prefer to spend your time as an artist?**

a. Marketing and promoting my work (4 points)

b. Networking with other artists and galleries (3 points)

c. Engaging with my audience on social media (2 points)

d. Creating without distractions (1 point)

4. **How do you envision your future as an artist?**

a. Being financially stable and able to focus solely on my art (4 points)

b. Having my work displayed in prestigious galleries (3 points)

c. Building a large, dedicated community of followers (2 points)

d. Creating meaningful art that fulfills me personally (1 point)

5. **What is your current approach to marketing your art?**

a. I actively sell and promote my work through multiple channels (4 points)

b. I network with galleries and attend art events (3

points)

c. I focus on building my social media presence (2 points)

d. I mostly focus on creating and let marketing happen when it can (1 point)

Scoring and Interpretations

16-20 Points: Financial Focus

You're driven by financial success and see your art career as a business. You're motivated to make a living from your work and enjoy the challenge of selling and marketing.

Moving Forward: Focus on developing multiple income streams—whether through selling originals, prints, or licensing your work. Prioritize marketing and sales channels that align with your financial goals, such as online art markets, print-on-demand services, or direct sales through your website. Make time for business planning, pricing strategies, and continuous promotion, but don't forget to balance your creative practice.

11-15 Points: Recognition and Prestige

Your goal is to gain recognition and establish a reputation in the art world. You're focused on getting your work into galleries and receiving accolades.

Moving Forward: Focus on networking within the art world. Build relationships with galleries, curators, and collectors who can help elevate your visibility. Apply for exhibitions, competitions, and residencies to showcase your work in prestigious venues. Cultivate a professional online presence that showcases your portfolio, and consider press outreach or collaborating with art influencers to build your reputation.

6-10 Points: Community and Audience Building

You love connecting with people through your art and thrive on building an engaged audience. Social media and online interactions are key to your success.

Moving Forward: Prioritize growing and nurturing your online community. Focus on platforms where your audience is most active, such as Instagram or TikTok, and experiment with engaging content like behind-the-scenes videos, livestreams, and polls. Consider setting up a newsletter or Patreon account to create a more personal connection with your followers and turn them into loyal supporters.

5 Points or Fewer: Personal Fulfillment

For you, success is about personal satisfaction. You're less concerned with external validation and more focused on the joy of creating meaningful art.

Moving Forward: Embrace your creative process and focus on producing work that brings you personal satisfaction. It's okay to prioritize your own fulfillment over commercial success. However, if you do want to share your work, consider small, intimate ways to connect with others, such as local exhibitions or an artist blog that allows you to reflect on your practice. Your authenticity will naturally attract like-minded people who appreciate your work.

Stay Connected and Share Your Feedback

As an independent author, your support means the world to me! Your feedback not only helps me continue creating and sharing valuable content with artists like you, but it also helps other readers discover my work. If you found this book helpful or inspiring, I'd be incredibly grateful if you could take a moment to follow me and leave a rating or review on your favorite platform.

- Amazon Author Central: **https://t.ly/ASBBJ** – Discover my latest books and updates.
- BookBub: **https://t.ly/sIjDG** – Get notified about new releases and special offers.
- Goodreads: **https://t.ly/VuqQy** – Connect with me and join in on book discussions.
- IndieBound: **https://t.ly/nqxOz** – Support independent bookstores while leaving feedback.

www.ingramcontent.com/pod-product-compliance
Lightning Source LLC
Chambersburg PA
CBHW071238050326
40690CB00011B/2169